More Praise for *A Woman's Guide to Claiming Space*

"If a book was a hug, a high five, and a help session all in one, it would be Eliza VanCort's book. VanCort shares her hard-earned lessons and heart-filled advice in this intersectional guidebook that will help women empower themselves and become 'good-ish' allies to others. I will be sharing it with my students, friends, and daughters."
—**Dolly Chugh, author of *The Person You Mean to Be* and Associate Professor, New York University Stern School of Business**

"This book digs deep into how we can bravely 'claim space' at work—physically through posture and voice—but also emotionally, behaviorally, and energetically by creating the types of networks and connections that break glass ceilings and elevate us. All of these aspects of power and bravery are essential if we want to live and work as we dream to. This powerful, comprehensive guide book is for every woman and every leader who wishes to access concrete tools to stop apologizing for being human, for being herself, or for things that aren't her fault, and to claim her space in the world while owning her own worthiness to achieve her ultimate potential."
—**Kathy Caprino, Career and Leadership Coach, Senior Forbes Contributor, author of *The Most Powerful You* and host of the Finding Brave podcast**

"A combination of big ideas and concrete, actionable advice, this powerful guidebook delivers transformative value to women in their twenties and thirties striving to make our mark and make a difference in the world. It's the road map we wish we had when launching our careers and a critical call to action for women to unite across differences to drive change."
—**Octavia Abell and Kyleigh Russ, cofounders of Govern for America and *Forbes* 30 Under 30 honorees**

"As a father who values self-sufficiency, confidence, and strength, I'll be giving this book to my teenage daughters! It's absolutely a must-read!"
—**Joe De Sena, founder and CEO, Spartan Race, and bestselling author of *Spartan Up!* and *Spartan Fit!***

"Women who want to be their most empowered selves both at home and at work, while raising up the women around them, must read this book!"
—**Christine Guest, Associate Professor, Ithaca College; Emmy-nominated filmmaker; and producer of the award-winning documentary *The Women of Titmouse Animation***

"Women of every race and background who want to claim space confidently and unapologetically will find concrete answers and edifying inspiration. Challenging, motivating, and transformative."
—**Misty Monroe, actor, educator, and creator of the award-winning, critically acclaimed one-woman show *Unapologetically Black***

"This book is as warm, authentic, empathetic, funny, and edifying as Eliza's (in-person) talks and seminars. I respect Eliza's works, and more importantly, the students I work with in higher education have truly benefited from her transformative practical advice, tools, and resources for years. With this important book, the world has access to her as well."
  —**DiOnetta Jones Crayton, Associate Dean and Director, Office of Minority Education, Massachusetts Institute of Technology**

"There are those that consciously or unconsciously try to diminish the voices of women as well as Black, Indigenous, and other people of color of any gender. Eliza presents us with powerful and practical strategies we can use to be our own champions and better champions of others as we individually and collectively claim our space to be heard."
  —**Sara Xayarath Hernández, Associate Dean for Inclusion and Student Engagement, Cornell University Graduate School**

"This welcome book is a warm, funny, and genuinely edifying resource that combines big ideas with real-world strategies. VanCort seamlessly emphasizes both transformative individual growth and the power of intersectional engagement."
  —**Andrew Chignell, PhD, Laurence S. Rockefeller Professor, University Center for Human Values, Princeton University, and Codirector, Hope and Optimism project**

"As a non-binary trans person who has dedicated my life to educating people about gender diversity, it was refreshing to see a book that does not rigidly define gender and does not exclude all but the White straight cis woman from the conversation. The advice VanCort gives is often universal, will help people of all genders help themselves, and perhaps more importantly, will help each of us amplify each other."
  —**Shelley Roth, entrepreneur, consultant, and five time author, including, *A Field Guide to Gender Neutral Language* and *Don't Call Me "Ma'am"***

"Eliza VanCort is on a mission to empower every woman to claim her space. With insightful wisdom and actionable advice, she shows you how to be seen and heard with confidence and to embrace that there is enough room for every woman to succeed. Eliza shows you how to take power and seed power to honor intersectionality and claim space for all women. I'm gifting her book to my women friends and colleagues—this is a must read!'"
  —**Caroline Dowd-Higgins, author of *This Is Not the Career I Ordered* and *Thrive Where You Are*, host of Your Working Life podcast**

"This is a must read for every college-aged woman who wants real guidance on how to be a real, kick-ass woman."
  —**Kieren Munson-Burke, college student**

A Woman's Guide to Claiming SPACE

STAND TALL. RAISE YOUR VOICE. BE HEARD.

Eliza VanCort

Foreword by
Alma Derricks,
former CMO of Cirque du Soleil RSD

BK
Berrett–Koehler Publishers, Inc.

Berrett-Koehler Publishers, Inc.
1333 Broadway, Suite 1000
Oakland, CA 94612-1921
Tel: (510) 817-2277
Fax: (510) 817-2278
www.bkconnection.com

ORDERING INFORMATION

Quantity sales. Special discounts are available on quantity purchases by corporations, associations, and others. For details, contact the "Special Sales Department" at the Berrett-Koehler address above.

Individual sales. Berrett-Koehler publications are available through most bookstores. They can also be ordered directly from Berrett-Koehler: Tel: (800) 929-2929; Fax: (802) 864-7626; www.bkconnection.com.

Orders for college textbook / course adoption use. Please contact Berrett-Koehler: Tel: (800) 929-2929; Fax: (802) 864-7626.

Distributed to the U.S. trade and internationally by Penguin Random House Publisher Services.

Berrett-Koehler and the BK logo are registered trademarks of Berrett-Koehler Publishers, Inc.

Printed in the United States of America

Berrett-Koehler books are printed on long-lasting acid-free paper. When it is available, we choose paper that has been manufactured by environmentally responsible processes. These may include using trees grown in sustainable forests, incorporating recycled paper, minimizing chlorine in bleaching, or recycling the energy produced at the paper mill.

Cataloging-in-Publication Data is available at the Library of Congress.

Library of Congress Control Number: 2021930254

ISBN: 9781523092734

First Edition

27 26 25 24 23 22 21   10 9 8 7 6 5 4 3 2 1

Book producer and text designer: Happenstance Type-O-Rama
Cover designer: Lynn Buckley
Cover art: Photo by Barbara Ann Jordan assisted by David Burbank

Mary Louise Marini VanCort
was a brilliant writer.
Her life was cut short.
Her story was never told.
She told me I could do anything.
I claim this space for her.
Thank you, Mom.

CONTENTS

PART 5: CLAIM SPACE UNITED

FOREWORD

A WOMAN'S GUIDE TO CLAIMING SPACE is the empowering, honest, and no-nonsense how-to manual that I wish I'd had on my nightstand twenty-five years ago. And again fifteen years ago. And once more about six months ago. Eliza has lived many lives, claimed many spaces, and helped countless women embrace their superpowers. With uncommon wisdom, grace, and grit, she brings a hug-kick-thunderclap that every woman needs in her life. Again and again and again.

Before I ran away and joined the circus, I considered myself a pretty sharp, savvy, and accomplished executive. Over two decades, I'd seen entire industries come and go. I'd built new businesses for some of the most beloved brands in the world. With raucous stories to share about Klingons, Blue Men, Dilbert, Snoopy, and even Chuck D, I was accustomed to being a pretty captivating cocktail party guest. But in the shiny, raunchy, and otherworldly fishbowl of Las Vegas, all of my resolve, my wits, and even my physical well-being would be stressed to the limit.

Under the big top, I discovered an odd metaphorical kinship with the extraordinary artists I was honored to call my colleagues. Contortionists' impossible backbends seemed startlingly familiar; so did the breathless high stakes of the high wire, stilt walking, juggling, plate spinning, sword swallowing, and fire breathing.

Definitely fire breathing.

It was my father who first taught me to inhale and exhale fire. Because he didn't have the words to tell me otherwise, he taught me the exact lessons he would have shared with a son: how to be brave, outspoken, ambitious, and more than a little conspicuous. Because I am my father's child, I ultimately soared to heights I never could have imagined in those early years. But because I am my father's *brown* and *female* child, I had to learn for myself that presenting with such force wasn't always welcome.

Despite his very best intentions, this is the part that he couldn't completely understand: building a meaningful life and living is tricky enough, but for a woman, like Ginger Rogers waltzing with Fred Astaire, doing it backward and in high heels is a bitch.

Space claiming is not for the faint of heart. And, depending on how many matching pieces of luggage you happen to be carrying with you—and the height of your sassy stilettos—the road can be long, narrow, and very steep. I perpetually carry the heaviest pieces strapped to my back. Other pieces at least have a wheel or two so I can drag them behind me with a little less effort. And, without question, there are many others who carry a much heavier load than I ever will. But the fundamental challenges that A WOMAN'S GUIDE TO CLAIMING SPACE addresses are universal. And Eliza's blessedly practical life lessons are right on time.

In a small world, standing tall is a threat. Daring to live out loud and question norms can activate intense opposition, fear, and jealousy from both men and, regrettably, other women. Stand tall anyway.

In a chauvinist world, raising your voice is an affront. Refusing to accept suffocating limitations will inevitably be branded destabilizing, immoral, and even dangerous. Raise your voice anyway.

And at a moment when we need the boldest, most compassionate, and supremely kick-ass leaders we can find, making yourself heard isn't really optional. A restless and desperate world is waiting for you to unfurl your cape and answer the call.

Among many other passions, Eliza and I share a reverence for Maya Angelou. As you stake your claim to your space, it's only fitting to center her powerful voice: "Each of us has that right, that possibility, to invent ourselves daily. If a person does not invent herself, she will be invented."

Throw your head back. Strike a pose. And never ever let yourself be silenced.

ALMA DERRICKS
Former CMO, Cirque du Soleil RSD
Founder of REV
Los Angeles, California
August 14, 2020

INTRODUCTION

Unapologetic Bravery: How to Fly without a Cape

Be your own hero, and claim space without apology.

When I dare to be powerful, to use my strength in the service of my vision, then it becomes less and less important whether I am afraid.

—AUDRE LORDE

For years I was afraid to be my own hero. I was waiting for someone, anyone, to fly out of the sky, à la Superman in that first movie with Christopher Reeve, and scoop me up . . . just like Lois Lane! (She was so pretty! I wanted to be *just* like her!) Eventually, however, I began to question if this was a solid and stable life strategy. Waiting for Superman to emerge from the sky and take you on a joyride, when you have zero flying skills yourself, is problematic . . . to say the least. What if he has to drop you off somewhere because there's some sort of crisis? You really have no control over *where* Superman drops you before flying off to save the world. And not only are you stuck in some random place, say Antarctica, but you can't really help him solve the crises. So, Superman will go off and have exciting adventures without you. He will set the terms of which crises get priority and how to solve them. He'll be the hero. Meanwhile, you'll be freezing your ass off with a bunch of penguins, praying he'll remember to come get you when he's done. Eventually I came to this conclusion: Nah. Lois can have him.

After reconsidering my dreams of being Lois, I decided if I wanted to fly like a superhero, I would have to become one myself. Until I was in my forties, I didn't fully understand my biggest barrier. It wasn't that I didn't come from Amazonia, or that I had no cape—although both would be total badassery. The barrier I faced could be summed up in two words.

Claiming Space

To claim space is to live the life of your choosing unapologetically and bravely. It is to live life the way you've always wanted. Your choices become yours. Your life is yours. To claim space is to never apologize for being the rule-breaking, rule-making badass/superhero/boss lady that you are. Not once. Not ever.

How I Cracked the Code to Claiming Space (Hint: Don't Text and Drive)

By the time I was a teenager, I had become a pretty damn good communicator, but I was also a master of ceding space. Somewhere deep down I believed that to stay safe, my true self had to stay invisible, so I used tactics women have been taught are acceptable. I flirted. I acted dumber than I was. I stated my opinion with apologies and questions. I often waited patiently for "my turn" to talk, while the young men at the table talked over me with impunity. I was getting the job done, but I was shrinking, losing a small piece of my power with every victory.

Then something miraculous happened. A car slammed into my head while I was riding my bike. I fully realize you may be thinking right now that I'm a bit nuts. Isn't getting hit in the head with a car a bad thing? Well, yes, it was. Indeed, it was really bad for a while. But it ended up being a good thing too—it transformed my life.

Here's what happened: The driver, while texting and driving, ran a red light. (Please don't text while you're supposed to be driving. Not ever.) After the car hit my body, I was thrown onto the hood, my head smashing into the hard metal. Then, unconscious, I bounced off her car like a rag doll, into the air, and landed on the ground. That's when I smashed the other side of my head on the asphalt. I woke up with a bilateral brain injury and bleeding in my head, otherwise known as a subdural hematoma. My world was turned upside down.

The oddest thing about what happened was how strangely everyone acted toward me. When people stopped behaving quite so peculiarly, I asked my dear friend about it: "Kim, why is everyone acting *so* weird?" Her answer shocked me. Everyone else wasn't acting weird; I was.

I had been talking painfully slowly and my once-rich vocabulary was basically gone. I was terrified. All my passions, all my work, had involved my communication skills, and now I couldn't communicate. My mother, once a brilliant poet, writer, and beloved English teacher, had developed paranoid schizophrenia in her late twenties—trapped in her own mind. My deepest fear was that something might go wrong with my brain—it was my waking nightmare. Now, I was living it.

My intuition had always guided my communication. The accident seemed to have knocked that right out of my head. If I wanted my life back, I would have to rebuild my communication skills by meticulously breaking them down into component parts and then mindfully rebuilding from the ground up, brick by brick.

I began to watch . . . everything. Why are some people heard and others ignored? What makes a sentence compelling? How do people cede power? Take power? Make people happy? Scare people? How do they inspire?

I tired easily, so watching wasn't as terrible as it would have been before my accident. When groups of dear friends visited, my ability to keep talking eventually faded. That's when I would watch. During my solitary moments, I researched voraciously.

Then the day came when I could finally tolerate leaving my house. I'd always loved people watching, but I did it more closely now, analyzing every tiny detail.

That woman sitting quietly in the coffee shop, sipping tea and reading the *Times* . . . why didn't anyone approach her? What signs did she give off that allowed her to read in peace? And that equally attractive woman at the table next to her . . . seemingly doing the same thing. Why did she have to fend off two men who tried to strike up unwanted conversations within a span of only twenty minutes? And why did it take her so long to shut each of them down?

I thought, and I watched, and I questioned, and I read, and I thought some more. The women who fared best in work and in life were, without question, masters at claiming space. But what did that mean?

At first I didn't have a full understanding of what that meant; I just knew "claiming space" kept popping into my mind. The fiercer, more successful, and happier a woman was, the more of a badass space claimer she was. What was the one quality that allowed a woman to be visible without apology, to claim space like it was her damn job? There had to be a magic bullet, one simple, clear answer for how to do it. Eventually, I came to this inevitable conclusion: there wasn't. That would have been great! But alas, we live in the real world, a world with complex problems calling for real, nuanced, and innovative solutions.

In the end, I figured out space-claiming queens understand the importance of five distinct qualities.

CLAIM PHYSICAL SPACE: BOW TO NO ONE!

Communicate powerfully with your voice and your body.

To claim space is to have great posture and speak with confidence. Know where your body is in space, always. The story your physicality and voice tells can clearly project confidence and strength.

CLAIM SPACE COLLABORATIVELY: AMPLIFY EACH OTHER!

Forge relationships that uplift you.

Claiming space is not a solitary activity. Carefully attend to your friendships, cultivate your professional relationships, lean on other women, and help other women. Create and nurture effective, powerful "old girl" networks.

NEVER CEDE YOUR SPACE: NEUTRALIZE YOUR KRYPTONITE!

Stop damaging patterns of self-sabotage.

Claiming space requires more than the physical. It means looking carefully at your past, identifying and knowing your pain points. Are you susceptible to dangerous, toxic relationships? Do you have impostor syndrome? Gaining an understanding of what can bring you to your knees will allow you to work toward never self-sabotaging again.

CLAIM SAFETY IN ANY SPACE: SHUT IT DOWN!

Thwart aggressors and protect yourself.

Claiming space means refusing to put up with interruptions, mansplaining, microaggressions, and other behaviors. You can achieve this in different ways—by cultivating an ally or through direct intervention yourself, you can learn how to shut them down.

CLAIM SPACE UNITED: COMMIT TO INTERSECTIONALITY!

Create a better world for us all.

Unless you are claiming space for all women, you are not claiming space. It demands solidarity and unity. Approach work and life with an open mind and heart. Listen to, believe, and advocate for other women. When we rise together, we rise so much higher.

A full life is a life of continuous discovery, growth, and change. Wise women understand they can never really master all of the five qualities. Instead, they accept their shortcomings while at the same time striving to achieve mastery. These women are unstoppable forces. Their ability to powerfully claim space serves as their anchor during life's inevitable storms and their wings when taking flight, reaching for the impossible.

Claim space without apology and you are a damn superhero—a fierce woman in control who makes things happen.

The How-To

These five categories are powerful umbrella concepts for more granular life challenges. For example, take physicality/voice. You can't just tell someone, "Hey, go out and claim physical space and use your voice like Beyoncé! *Good luck!*" The component parts of control over your body and voice must be broken down, understood, and mastered: posture, voice, physicality, messaging, and phrasing. Once you master those skills, however, you will own that category. A macrolevel discussion of each category and explicit, detailed how-to advice on those granular changes are what this book is all about.

Deep down, each of us once believed we could do anything, just like the boys. When we were little girls, we imagined a world that would receive us on our merits, a world that would be fair, a world that would never ask us to be small, to shrink, to diminish ourselves to survive. Time, and the world, showed us a different truth. Yet we continue to work for that world we imagined for ourselves, because giving up is not an option. And each time one woman is knocked down, gets back up again, refuses to become invisible, we all become a little wiser, a little stronger. We come a little closer to that world. We must work to throw out the rules that held our grandmothers and mothers down. We must fight to rewrite those rules so they never hold us or our daughters down. A world where every woman can claim space without apology or fear is a world worth fighting for.

Conversations in the Bathroom

I was going to call this book *Conversations in the Bathroom*. The women's bathroom, which tragically is still not universally open to our trans sisters, can be a space like no other, transforming strangers into trusted old friends, lowering our guard in ways unthinkable at bus stops or cocktail parties. After giving my talks, when my mic has been turned off, leadership has shaken my hand one last time, and my work has officially "ended," the second Q&A in the bathroom invariably begins. It can be cramped, and often it smells like, well, a bathroom, but none of us seem to notice. Experiences are shared and questions are asked. It's been such an honor to hear every last story from each exceptional woman, even if it means almost missing my flight home on the regular. My bathroom Q&A record is almost two hours . . . I didn't regret a minute of it.

Yet I understand the reason we have to huddle in the bathroom is that so many of us don't feel safe claiming space outside of it. Until women, as a collective, master the five ways to claim space, we never will. (This includes raising our voices against the exclusion of our trans sisters from women's bathrooms. When any woman is unsafe in a space, we all lose.)

This book is a detailed guide to space claiming, which is a hell of a lot more rewarding, fun, and empowering than freezing your ass off in Antarctica with penguins, waiting for Superman to save you. It will empower us all to stand tall in the face of fear, raise our united voices, and be heard even in situations that traditionally would silence us. It was inspired by my journey and informed research, and created for all women. It owes a lot to my clients' experiences, and those wonderful moments throughout the world I've spent huddled around a bathroom sink, engaging in real sister-to-sister talk. I wrote it envisioning a busy woman going to the index and saying, "Damn, I'm struggling with [insert space-claiming issue] today. I know there's got to be a chapter on this!" And lo and behold, there it is! She reads the chapter, making a few mental notes about how and when she'll apply her new skills. Soon after, she walks into work in her full power.

I hope you enjoy reading the book as much as I loved writing it. And if you do, please claim some space and pass it on to other women committed to stepping fully into their most badass selves without fear or apology.

The Firsts

Women who are best at claiming space are our real-life super-heroes. They are our Oprahs, Kamala Harrises, Sandra Day O'Connors, Alexandria Ocasio-Cortezes, Ruth Bader Ginsburgs, and Maya Angelous. They are our Firsts . . . the First CEO of this company, the First mayor of that town, the First woman in her family to start a business, the First daughter in her family to attend college, the First women who said #MeToo . . . We point to these women and say, "She did it! It's possible. And if she can do it, then maybe I can too!"

If we're lucky, one of our everyday heroes, one of the Firsts in our lives, will believe in us. "Of course you can!" she'll say to us. "What will your First be? I can't wait to see it! What are you waiting for?" And we will listen.

We can all be "the First," whatever that may mean to us. We can claim space with courage and empathy and conviction, breaking rules and making new ones. We are not meant to be earthbound, freezing our asses off in Antarctica, waiting for some guy in a cape to save yet another cat in a damn tree. We are far more fierce and strong and brave and capable than that.

The best part is, when we claim space for ourselves, we can turn around and see the other women struggling like we once did and reach out our hands to them, arms outstretched. We can reach for our daughters, girlfriends, coworkers, or sometimes even perfect strangers; we can be empowered enough that we know how to help other women claim space. We can complete the cycle of sisterhood, because we know when we rise together, we rise so much higher.

So put on your damn cape, learn to fly, and go save your own life.

No more waiting. The time to claim space is now.

How to Get the Most out of This Book

BIG IDEA: EMBRACE THE LESSON

Sometimes we run from lessons because we don't want to think the thought, "Damn, I wish I had known this sooner! I wasted so much time!"

Fear of wasting time is one of the best ways to waste your life. It is a counterproductive mindset.

My brilliant friend and mentor Kim Munson-Burke is a gifted therapist, but I like to think of her as Yoda/Morpheus. She once said to me, "I don't believe in the concept of wasting time. You can't waste time, unless you don't learn and grow from your experiences." Had I not learned to reframe my ideas about time, I would have missed critical lessons.

As you read this book, remember that every lesson you learn, every time you realize you could have done something differently, you have not wasted time. When you learn what you could have done differently, you are saving time, because you're saving your future.

You can't find heaven if you've shackled yourself to a road in hell.

Read It like You Want To!

Make this book work for you! There is no "right way" to read it! This book was written for real women who live busy lives. Each woman faces different challenges, and sometimes they change from day to day. While each part of this book builds on the last, each section of each chapter is also able to stand alone. There are days you may "need" to read one chapter out of order. Do it! Skipping around isn't cheating!

Using this book in a way that best fits your life isn't cheating. Quite the opposite. It's a pretty space-claiming thing to do.

PART 1

CLAIM PHYSICAL SPACE

Bow to No One!

Claim physical space with your voice and your physicality.

And where she stood, she stood tall.
—THE LUMINEERS

We all know that woman who walks into a room and just has that something that turns heads. It's not necessarily that she's gorgeous or rich or famous, although let's face it, those things don't hurt. Primarily, it has to do with how she carries herself. We also may know people who might be beautiful or rich or famous who make themselves small, almost blending in with the walls.

A large part of how men command respect is physically and vocally. They claim massive amounts of space like it's their damn job. This goes well beyond manspreading and taking both arm-rests. Women have been given the message that if we take up too much space with our bodies and voices, we are impolite, over-stepping, or—gasp!—unladylike. This, of course, is a setup. If we don't claim space, we are invisible. If we do, we are too confident, strident, bitchy, or bossy.

The chapters in this part will teach you how to claim space by harnessing the power of both your body and your voice while inoculating yourself against damaging pushback.

To claim physical space for yourself is to claim the armrests—at least one of them! Allow your shoulders to expand rather than contract, and use your voice in ways that say in no uncertain terms that, when you speak, you deserve to be heard.

I have two careers that I love. I teach communication skills, and I run an acting studio specializing in the Sanford Meisner tech-nique, which is all about the minutiae of human behavior and the nuances of communication. My acting students are consistently dumbstruck by how transformative a simple postural adjustment feels. I've also seen women in my communication workshops cry with relief after unlocking the power of their voices. The way we move in space is deeply rooted in our history. *The way we carry our-selves has a profound impact on who we are, and on our emotional life.*

A Personal History

Claiming space with my body and voice has been one of the most challenging, and most transformative, experiences of my life. My childhood was tumultuous, thanks in no small part to my mother's paranoid schizophrenia. By the time I turned five, I was a hesitant, scared little girl. I spent a lot of my time alone, hunched over, quietly hiding behind my long curtain of thick, wavy, black hair, only peeking out occasionally. I lived life as if I were sneaking a look at a scary movie, waiting for the jump cut.

I telegraphed a message like a big neon sign with my body language: "I'm really scared and I'm damaged. Please pretend I'm invisible."

As was apt to happen, kids read my sign and honored my wishes, steering far clear of me. So I was a lonely little girl, spending a lot of time surreptitiously watching other kids have fun together while I played make-believe solo with my dolls. Yet, deep down, I just didn't feel like this was me. At school I'd watch my classmates laugh and play and scream with glee on the playground. I still remember how much I wanted to be one of them!

Then one day in fourth grade, two little girls skipped up to me while I was alone on the swings at recess. "We saw you were playing by yourself and wondered if you wanted to play with us."

It felt like something out of a movie—I almost expected the heavens to open up while the music swelled and really flattering, warm sunlight hit our cheeks. This moment would change everything! I wanted to say, "Yes, yes, yes, I do! Thank you, thank you, *thank you* for asking!" Instead I looked away shyly and said in an almost inaudible whisper, "Yes, I'd like that." With that, they both moved to either side of me and climbed onto the swings. As I swung higher and higher, sandwiched between my utterly perfect new friends, I was convinced they were saving my terrible fourth grade life. They sort of did.

I recently reconnected with one of those friends, Joan Ramage MacDonald. Joan is Professor MacDonald now, and she is still an exceptional human. She had no idea how impactful her seemingly small act of kindness had been.

Joan didn't know that the moment she and Joanna pulled me into their little circle of thoughtful, caring girls was the moment

I began to learn how to make friends and be a friend. But it had made a huge difference, and after that my confidence slowly grew.

I pulled my hair back enough to see just a little better. I stood up just a little straighter. I smiled more. I laughed out loud. I ran to the swings at recess, rather than walking quietly along the fence, hoping I didn't bump into anyone. Eventually I started to appear on the outside like the person I felt I could be on the inside. I became more confident, and my body and voice reflected that confidence to the world. While all of this was happening, my parents put me in therapy. I can point to Joanna and Joan, and years of therapy, as the two pivotal events on my journey to presenting to the world as the woman I wanted to be.

If you have a critical meeting, or a career-altering keynote, or an interview for your dream job in a week or even a month, you don't have time to wait for a Joan or Joanna to save you, and therapy takes years. In high-stakes situations like these, quick and effective solutions are needed.

Here's the fascinating thing I discovered as an actor, and more dramatically as an acting teacher and communication coach: *you can do this process in the opposite order, and with markedly faster results.* You don't have to feel more confident on the inside to look more confident on the outside. Learn to present with authority, and even if initially you don't feel that way, you will be transformed.

The reason for this is twofold:

1. **Our physicality and our emotional life are deeply interconnected.** Externally present confidence and power, and in short order you will feel better internally.

2. **People treat you the way they perceive you.** When you present more powerfully and confidently, you will be perceived that way by others. Act like you're scared, and they'll treat you like you're weak and fragile. Act with authority and you'll be treated with respect.

The chapters in this part will give you concrete tools to transform your external self—your physicality and voice. This will change the way you're received and, in turn, treated by others.

This stuff is powerful, and it works.

I have seen client after client transform their entire lives after learning just one of the skills from these chapters. Women who couldn't get hired have received multiple offers after changing their approach to a handshake. Self-proclaimed "terrible negotiators" have negotiated huge deals, or higher pay, with a combination of mirroring and vocal adjustments. And women who weren't taken seriously suddenly have found themselves heard and respected after a simple postural reset.

Learning to claim space confidently and effectively with your body and your voice is straightforward and easy to understand. That said, adopting these skills may not feel comfortable at first. That's OK—just dive in and practice. Eventually, you will move from "This feels like it's just not me" to "Oh my God, I finally feel like the total space-claiming boss lady I've been working to be."

POSTURE

A Brief History of My Breasts

In fourth grade I began developing breasts at seemingly lightning speed. I legitimately worried my breasts would grow so huge that one day, whilst walking the busy halls of my middle school, I would lose my balance and tumble forward, my books and my hopes of ever being cool simultaneously crashing down around me. (Thankfully, this did not happen. I never did, however, achieve my goal of being a cool middle schooler.) Going from flat chested to curvy, on top of being taller than almost all of the other girls, made me feel deeply, profoundly uncomfortable in my own skin. To hide my body, and to be shorter and smaller than the boys, I began to stand a bit like that creepy, scraggly white-haired guy in *The Rocky Horror Picture Show*.

Thankfully, years later, I happened upon a two-year acting program in the Sanford Meisner technique, the technique I fell in love with and have spent most of my career teaching. I wasn't slumping like *The Rocky Horror Picture Show* guy at this point, but my posture wasn't stellar. My Meisner class was a posture game changer. Meisner teaches something called "physical adjustments" to help actors create a character.

Physical Adjustments

A person changes something *external* about herself (body or voice), triggering a radical *internal* change (inner emotional life).

I soon discovered that the characters I worked on in class with good posture always felt more confident. This happened predictably, no matter the character. Once I figured this out, I decided I wanted to live my life feeling that way and began standing straight not just on stage, but off.

The impact was immediate and staggering. Men did not harass me as much on the streets. I was interrupted less. I was even given more time in auditions! Overall, I was simply treated better and with more respect. My subsequent confidence boost created a wonderful feedback loop. Stand straight, get more respect, work even harder to stand straight consistently. Rinse. Repeat.

I've kept up my good posture ever since, and I have no doubt my posture is part of why people tell me I project authority. Now I border on obnoxious when it comes to preaching about better posture. Change your posture, and both your body and self-esteem will thank you. Change your posture, change your life!

Why Posture Matters: The Basics

Posture isn't just about your back. It isn't just about your body. It's about *you*—how you feel about yourself and how the world sees you. When I work with clients, I sometimes only need to adjust their posture to radically alter how they are received and, more importantly, how they feel. This is why all aspiring space-claiming women must stand tall!

If you have poor posture, read on to learn tools to improve. If your posture is already good, fantastic! I promise this will up your game.

Let's start with the facts. Posture impacts us in ways that go far beyond body mechanics. Check out this illustration.[1]

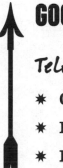

GOOD POSTURE	POOR POSTURE
Telegraphs	**Telegraphs**
* Confidence	* Insecurity
* Power	* Weakness
* Decisiveness	* Tentativeness
* Happiness	* Depression
Health Benefits	**Health Drawbacks**
* Stronger core muscles	* Poor breath support
* Increased energy	* Increased fatigue
* Improved circulation	* Compromised gut health
* Upbeat outlook	* Depression
* Less abnormal wear on joints	* Joint stress
* Better sleep	* Sleep disorders
* Better gut health	* Incontinence, constipation, heartburn

   The first step to having better posture is to stop behaviors that make your posture worse. There are five main habits that tend to unconsciously diminish your space-claiming capacity. These are movement patterns you probably engage in daily to some extent. Constantly engaging in these patterns has a cumulative effect, and building good habits where you currently have bad ones will result in better overall posture throughout your day. Even I don't avoid all of them. But you should. Thank you for tolerating my hypocrisy.

* **Lifting.** Don't bend with your back; bend with your legs. You may feel weird picking up your grocery bags off the ground like a weightlifter, but you will look even weirder hobbling around after throwing out your back.

* **Traveling.** Avoid slouching on long trips. This is hard to do, but slumping for hours on long flights is hard on your body. I suggest standing up and doing stretches in the aisle. People will 100 percent judge you, and you might not be able to pull it off on every flight. If you can't pull it off in the aisle, just walk to the bathroom a lot, paying particular attention to your posture. You'll get off that flight in 100 percent better shape than the people laughing about how uncool you are.

* **Cell phoning.** When talking on the phone or texting, hold up your phone; don't make your head tilt down to your phone.

* **Working.** If you're like me, you sit or work at your computer until you dehydrate and your back breaks. This is not optimal. Be sure to reset your posture regularly by setting a time to take breaks to stand up and take small walks. This is also a good excuse to network at the water cooler. If you're working from home, put on your headset and call a friend for a quick catch-up. It can be even easier to fall into a void of sitting for hours and hours in front of your laptop when you're home. Try not to fall into that trap. Set a timer if you have to, but get up and walk around.

* **High heeling.** Don't wear high heels. After a night of wearing a great pair of mules, our feet don't need studies to tell us high heels can be a rare form of torture. And there are studies . . . lots of them. Indeed, I searched for "study high heels and back pain," and in under a second 368,000,000-plus results popped

up. We *know* wearing very high heels is not the best thing for our posture . . . or our hips, back, knees, or Achilles tendon, for that matter. So don't wear them. They are bad. Bad, bad, bad!

Here's the truth: I have an embarrassing number of heels in my closet. The distinctive don't-mess-with-me click, click, click of a killer pair of stilettos always leaves me feeling fierce, yet all warm and fuzzy inside. And I love my new three-inch, fire-engine-red suede pumps. Delicious. If you are like me and can't give up your three-inch posture killers, try putting flip-flops in your purse for when you are in transit. Give your feet and your back a bit of a break!

Transform Your Posture in Just Three Steps and Only Five Minutes a Day!

Now you know standing tall is important, and you aren't slumped over your desk anymore. What's next? Learn to improve your posture with little time and effort. These simple exercises are easy to do, but don't expect them to have an immediate effect. Do them regularly, and you will start to improve without even noticing. Your biggest challenge will probably be reading through this next part. I tried to add some spice, but I will admit it's somewhat technical. Plow through it. You'll thank yourself later! (Please enjoy the goofy drawings of me demonstrating! You're welcome.)

STEP 1: ACTIVATE YOUR CORE

The first step to having excellent posture is, surprisingly, lying on the floor! Once you learn this, it will take less than a second to do it.

1. Lie down on a few towels or a thin mat.
2. Bend your knees, with your feet flat.
3. Suck your belly button up and in.

4. Check to see if the muscle on the inside of your pelvic bone is tight.

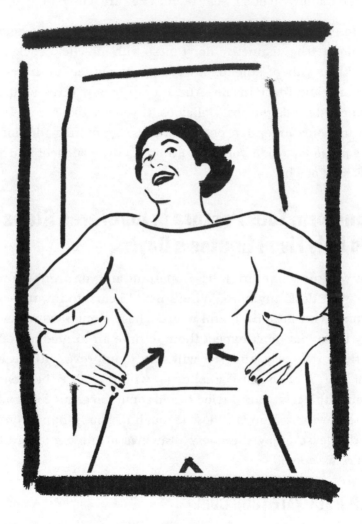

Practice doing this until you can easily activate your core when you're lying down. Once you can consistently and quickly activate your core lying down, try it standing up. Eventually you will be able to do this while walking and sitting. For me, sitting is the hardest. The temptation to crumple into any cozy chair is pretty overwhelming!

Once your core is activated, your posture will immediately start improving. When you start to notice this postural shift, it's time for the next step. It's a small but critical variation on the traditional shoulder roll.

STEP 2: SQUARE YOUR SHOULDERS

This takes about one minute, four times a day.
Start by activating your core, and then

1. Pull your shoulders up toward your ears.

2. Pull your shoulders way back *without rolling them down at all!*

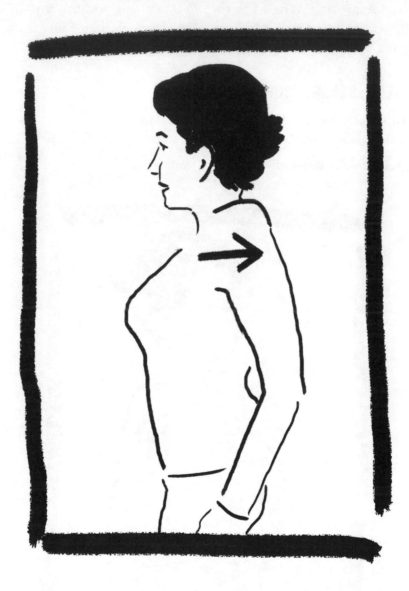

3. *Keeping your shoulders back,* push them down. (Your chest should feel way too far forward—think Madonna in her cone bra!)

4. Inhale deeply.

5. As you slowly exhale, stop actively pulling your shoulders back.

Where your shoulders land is your neutral position. You're done!

Do two repetitions four times a day. Be sure to reset during the day when you find yourself backsliding. (Yes, that was a pun.)

If you didn't find this last exercise difficult, skip to the posture deep dive. If you did find it hard, you may have tight pectoral muscles. The following go-to pec exercise can help.

STEP 3: STRETCH THOSE PECS

Many might think they don't need this. Most probably do. It takes about fifty-five seconds at most.

1. Stand next to a wall.
2. Put your palm on the wall.

3. Slide your hand up the wall.

4. Without bouncing, rotate your torso away from the wall to create a gentle stretch.

5. Do this on both arms.

If you felt a stretch when you did this, be sure to stretch before and after doing "square your shoulders" reps.

And you're done! You're a rock star worthy of standing like Captain Marvel that moment after she realized she had some *serious* powers. Fantastic!

Now, shifting gears, I know I said what you would learn would take just five minutes. If five minutes a day is about all you can devote to posture, I fully get it. What you learned here will suffice. No need to keep reading.

You kept reading! Great! Time for a deeper dive into your posture. The information below will elevate your posture while also globally improving your health. It will take time, but if you kept reading, you already know that it will be well worth it. I promise.

DEEP DIVE: HUGE REWARDS

Takes a lot more than five minutes but is so worth it!

Beyond the previous simple exercises, there are several other steps you can take to solidify your new and improved posture. It's a lot more work, but the payoff is huge. Find the one that sounds most appealing to you and fits with your schedule, and give it a try. There is no one-size-fits-all approach, so you might have to do some trial and error. You've found the right one for you when your posture doesn't just feel better, your body aches less and you feel more confident in your own skin.

* **The Alexander Technique.** The Alexander Technique has made a radical difference for my clients, especially folks with chronic back pain. The Alexander Technique fixes your posture systemically while also improving how your body moves in space. For more information, search online for Alexander Technique, your city, and your state. You can also learn more by searching for American Society for the Alexander Technique. It is well worth the investment! (These teachers must be certified. Don't work with anyone who isn't!)

* **Pilates.** Take up this LA favorite and you will have something in common with celebrities like Jamie Lee Curtis, Vanessa Williams, Hugh Grant, Kate Hudson, and Madonna. (I suspect

Wonder Woman, Supergirl, Storm, and Jessica Jones probably secretly take Pilates as well, but I have no evidence to prove it.) Many people associate Pilates with the machines and the corresponding price tag for those classes. But Pilates classes done on the floor, "Pilates mat" classes, are actually more challenging and truer to the original method developed by Joseph Pilates. Classes that use machines are useful for rehabilitation (their original purpose!) and for isolating small muscles. But classes on a mat cost the same as a yoga class, are more challenging, and will do just as much or more for your posture.

Several of my clients with chronic back pain have become pain free after committing to regular Pilates classes. Pilates strengthens your core muscles, helps you become mindful of good spinal alignment, and improves your flexibility. To find a good Pilates instructor, I recommend *not* going online. The quality of instruction can vary, and word of mouth is a lot more reliable than the internet. Pilates also helps with balance, which will allow you to move like Okoye in *Black Pan ther* during that incredible fight scene in the casino where she gives new meaning to claiming space. (OK, maybe you won't be just like her, as you haven't trained for years in Wakanda, but your balance will markedly improve.)

✳ **Weight lifting.** Hands down, this is my favorite. I weight train every other day, and I can't live without it! More importantly, weight lifting most predictably turns my clients' posture around while making them generally feel fiercer. Standing tall is easier when you're stronger, and lifting makes you strong! Some women are afraid of lifting weights, fearing it's going to make them look too "bulky." If you share this fear, get a personal trainer and let them know you want to get stronger, not bigger. It's best to have a trainer, but it's expensive. If you can't afford a personal trainer, just look for instructional videos online. There are countless videos on how to lift without bulking up. Ease in slowly and carefully using a reputable guide online, but please do give weight lifting a shot. With a safe, incremental approach, you'll begin to feel a lot like Wonder Woman in the last movie when she walks across no-man's-land.

Speaking of that movie, here's what Gal Gadot, who played Wonder Woman, told *Glamour* magazine about gaining seventeen pounds of muscle after strength training for the role: "I feel so much better now. When you feel strong, it changes everything— your posture, the way you walk. I look at photos from five years ago and think, whoa, I was too skinny. It's not cool." Wonder Woman, I couldn't have said it better.

Invest in Bowing to No One!

Spending time, energy, and sometimes money to cultivate better posture is an investment well worth making. Regardless of your height, you will be stunned at how differently you feel, and how differently you're treated. Never let your posture tell a story you don't want it to . . . or make you look like that creepy guy from *The Rocky Horror Picture Show*. In the immortal words of my hero Dr. Maya Angelou, "Stand up straight and realize who you are. That you tower over your circumstances."

VOICE

Your voice is a powerful tool. You can use it to scare, inspire, intimidate, or soothe. It can show strength, or reveal weakness, dilute an argument, or bolster a point. This chapter breaks down voice into its component parts so that your communication isn't left to intuition or chance. You will learn to control your voice and, by extension, the way you are received by others.

Women develop strategies in response to how we are received by the world that hurt us rather than help us. My dear, brilliant friend Dr. Leo Taylor works in the Office of Diversity, Equity, and Inclusion at The Ohio State University. Leo is a brilliant educator who can explain just about anything compellingly. Through his scholarship and lived experience, he's taught me so much over the years. Leo is also a transgender man.

To quote him directly, "I was assigned female at birth and later medically transitioned to masculinize my appearance so that it matches my gender identity. This gives me insights into gender, voice, and power others simply don't have. I've lived in both worlds."[1] In other words, Leo knows from experience how women and men are treated differently.

Years ago, I asked Leo what the most mind-blowing difference is between a world that viewed him as female and a world that recognizes him as male. I was so impacted by his answer,

I shared it in my TEDx, "Women, Power, and Revolutionizing Speech."

Here's what he said:

> Oh, that's easy. People, especially men, interrupt me less, listen to what I have to say more, and don't push back as much. When I'm in a meeting with women, I have to be careful. I start talking and all the women stop. I had no idea how much power and privilege I didn't have until I got it. It was shocking. And I'm not alone. I hear this again and again from trans men. If, like me, they pass as male, their voices become so much more heard. And trans women experience just the opposite.

Learning to control how you speak will not only help you claim space vocally but also contribute to disrupting systems that keep women small.

Lifting: Make Them Listen, Learn, and Remember

Whether you're giving a talk, in a social setting, or in a meeting, you want people to remember your most important point, and you want to be interesting. One of the best ways to do this is to figure out what part of a sentence or paragraph you really want people to remember and then "lift" it. Lifting is the intersection of volume and the art of power, persuasion, and inspiration . . . all wrapped up in one tidy word! Lifting technically means highlighting certain parts of a sentence or an idea by modulating physicality and voice.

If you lift well, *people will remember exactly what you want them to.*

Have you listened to a speaker and not been sure what the take-home message was? These folks don't know how to lift. Have lift, will influence. You, not your audience, should be in control of what message people walk away with.

Slow Down, Speed Up!

Varying your cadence, the speed of your speech, is a great way to lift.

We all remember that teacher or boss who bored us to tears because they were such terrible speakers. Varying your cadence also makes you a lot more interesting, and it inoculates you from being that teacher in *Ferris Bueller's Day Off*! Remember "Bueller . . . Bueller . . . Bueller . . ."? The reason we all laughed so hard at that point is because he never changed his cadence at all. We all relate to being trapped in front of a speaker who made us think, "Well, that was X minutes of my life I'll never get back."

You can make people remember anything you want about a sentence just by slowing down during the part of the sentence or paragraph you want people to remember. Indeed, people can come away with a radically different feeling about a sentence, and a completely different memory about what you were saying, simply because you slowed down.

Women, and Some Bad Advice

The key for women is *not* to listen to most communication advice about cadence. Many communication coaches advise people badly by saying all people should vary their cadence by going from slow to fast and fast to slow. The problem is women tend to have elevated speech patterns; in other words, we speak more quickly. So, when coaches talk about the benefits of "people" going from slow to fast, they're really talking about men. Most women who go from slow to fast are really going from fast to faster. Women who fall on the cadence bell curve should think about going from neutral to slow, so they don't run the risk of speaking too quickly. The last thing most of us need is to purposefully speed up!

Slowing down is hard for most women. All of our training runs counter to being slow. The reason for this has two component parts:

1. **We share the same allotted time to talk.** In conversation there is a socially acceptable amount of time to talk. If you

don't believe me, think about that person at a party. You know, *that* person. The one who is talking beyond his or her allotted time, rambling on and on and on while people get more and more annoyed or bored. If this person is incredibly powerful, people may tolerate them. If they're not, people will either find someone else to mingle with or interrupt them.

2. **We have to talk more to be believed.** The tricky part for women is that in professional settings, or most settings, for that matter, women have to offer a lot more evidence to be heard and believed. This causes quite the conundrum. *We have to fit more words into the same acceptable amount of time to speak.* The solution most women come up with is speaking very quickly. Unfortunately, speaking very quickly is a disempowering speech pattern!

Speaking slowly is a sign of confidence and owning your power. It's a way of vocally claiming space. Think about the most powerful people you know—I can almost guarantee that they don't speak incredibly quickly. They don't have to. People are willing to wait for them. If you can learn how to do this, you will automatically command more power. Speak like a boss, and you'll be treated like one.

Steps to Slowing Down

Here are some ideas to help you speak more slowly:

1. **Become cognizant of your cadence.** If you fall within the bell curve of most women's speech patterns, you are a slightly elevated talker, which means you need to slow down and never speed up on purpose for variation.

2. **Practice slowing down.** Say the sentence "Shaun I need to tell you something you're fired." Practice slowing down on different words (one or two) in that sentence. Notice what pops out

to you and how you feel different depending on which words you're lifting.

3. **Play and experiment.** Start practicing slowing down for emphasis in everyday life.

4. **Utilize eye contact.** As with silence, be sure that you are making direct eye contact while slowing down. If you look away, you may get interrupted.

Public speaking tip: When there's a place I want to slow down in a speech, I italicize that part to remind myself to do it when I practice. I'm much more likely to lift using slower cadence when I'm giving the actual speech if I have practiced several times well in advance.

Slowing down is one of those delicious tools that garners instant respect and isn't that difficult to learn. It might feel a little odd at first, but soon you'll find that people remember what you say more and tune in to your message more easily.

Volume: Speak Quietly So You Can Be Heard

Your volume tells a story. People with very soft voices appear meek. People with unusually loud voices can be seen as really obnoxious, especially by patrons in one of those snooty, fancy restaurants. The loudness or softness of your voice is one of the first things, besides a handshake, people notice about you.

Learn to control your volume and you can

1. Make people feel connected to you.

2. Ensure people remember the relevant points in your talk/ presentation/job interview.

3. Impact how people perceive you.

It's important to modulate your volume so you can persuade, inspire, and squeeze the most meaning out of your words.

Before Diving In

If you really struggle with decent projection, or have always felt you speak too softly, please don't ever think speaking with a good strong volume is something you are born with—good projection can absolutely be taught and it's never too late to learn! (To be clear, I'm not talking about yelling; I'm talking about speaking with your full voice engaged at standard conversational volume.) That said, any book that claims it can help you learn to project without privately coaching you or working with you in a workshop is misrepresenting itself. If your volume is so quiet you fall well off the bell curve, I strongly recommend you take a voice workshop or, better yet, enlist the help of a qualified voice teacher. (Call a college with a musical theater department to get a list of the best voice teachers. Never put your voice in jeopardy by hiring someone with second-rate skills.) Your voice teacher will help you learn proper breath support, better placement of your vocal box, easy-to-learn vocal massage, and all the skills you need for proper projection.

The one thing you may not need customized help with is breath support. Search for "instructional diaphragmatic breathing video" online. For a small number of people who struggle with projection, this may be all you need.

At Work: Elevate Your Baseline

In most public speaking settings, whether it be a meeting, a pitch to VCs (venture capitalists), a job talk, or a keynote, it's important to have a baseline volume that is louder than your usual voice.

Why?

When people are excited, they raise their volume. Volume that is a little louder makes audiences feel you're authoritative, fully engaged, and happy to be there. It also signals you're an authority.

Lifting: How to Do It with Volume

You can lift two ways using volume:

1. **Getting louder.** This simply means you *raise* your volume on the words people should remember. This is the most traditional way to lift. Think of Dr. Martin Luther King's classic "I Have a Dream" speech. As he was quoting a spiritual, "Free at last, free at last!" Dr. King's volume was much higher than in the rest of the speech. The crowd's cheers were deafening. Dr. King was a master of using volume to rouse crowds and make points. (Of course, he had a historically transformative message as well. That said, being such a brilliant speaker contributed to Dr. King's ability to powerfully convey his vision.)

2. **Getting quieter.** This simply means you *lower* your volume on the words people should remember. This works because, as human beings, we build intimacy by telling secrets. That's why even if you're alone in a room with someone, you lower your voice when sharing a secret. It's as if you're saying, "I'm sharing this secret just with you! Can't you tell by my lowered volume?" President Obama, who I will admit I have a major communication crush on, is a master at this. I love watching as he leans in, speaking to the crowd quietly. The crowd always responds in kind, leaning forward as if he is telling an important secret to them and only them. Spoiler: He's not. Obama is just being really quiet because he knows that being quiet fosters a feeling of one-on-one intimacy with his audiences. Either that, or he's a natural. I'm not sure which.

My favorite example of lifting by getting quieter came from a Professor Andrew Chignell, a client I was working with on his massive open online course, or MOOC. Andrew is a rock star in his field, philosophy. His beautifully resonant, loud voice allows him to lift ideas while teaching huge classes in gigantic lecture halls.

Andrew wanted to highlight a part of a sentence in the script for his MOOC. It was "human cost." When he first said the sentence, he said it like this (the bolded words were loud):

> What we haven't talked about yet [pause] **is the human cost of this kind of farming**.

I suggested Andrew get quieter, not louder, on the bolded part. He did, and the entire feeling of the sentence changed.

Now, you try the following example by quieting down on the bolded section:

> Yesterday I went to the store. [pause] **And I got milk. And I got eggs.**

Sounds like something very interesting happened with that milk and eggs, doesn't it?

You can make almost anything sound compelling if you start with a louder voice and then drop your volume.

Magnify Your Message by Minimizing Your Voice

Here are some suggestions for quieting down to lift an idea:

1. **Start strong.** Give yourself somewhere to go. Be sure your baseline volume is strong so you can get quieter without becoming inaudible.

2. **Calibrate for location.** Be sure your volume suits your venue.

   a. **One on one.** If you're with one person, match their volume.

   b. **Meetings.** If you're running a meeting, speak just a tad more loudly than conversational speech. (This will also help you command authority.)

   c. **Speeches.** If you're in a big lecture hall (with a mic), talk quite a bit more loudly than usual. Volume is space dependent, and everyone is different, so how loud this will be depends on you and the space. This is why pop stars yell "How you all doin'?" when they begin their shows. If they didn't yell, their high-tech speakers would be plenty loud enough, but because they yell, we feel as if they're making an effort to be heard and are really excited to be there. This builds good will with us while getting us excited about the night . . . and an excited audience is a wonderful audience!

d. **Not sure?** Aren't sure about how to modulate your volume for a certain space or circumstance? Watch the people around you who are excellent communicators and follow their lead. You can also record yourself trying sentences in different ways. Sometimes you think you are slowing down or speeding up or speaking loudly or softly . . . but you're not. You will hear it better if you listen outside of your own head.

3. **Pause.** Transitions, transitions, transitions! If you're going to quiet down to lift an idea, never barrel right into a lower volume. Always pause briefly before bringing your volume back down. Pauses draw focus to what you're saying while also preparing your listener for a tonal shift in your communication. If you don't pause, your volume shift can seem forced and jarring.

4. **Return!** One pitfall to dropping your volume is getting stuck there and forgetting to bring your volume back up again. This happens commonly with women used to being quiet in everyday life, or when someone feels out of their element in a leadership position.

After you have lifted the word or phrase you want people to remember, bump up your volume! This ensures you don't end up sounding quiet and timid. It also bookends your lift, which is important: if the lift goes on and on, it ceases to be a lift and morphs into "Wow, that person is quiet as hell."

Silence: Make Them Listen, or Save Yourself

Silence is one of my favorite tools to claim space. It is, without question, a powerful way to get your point across and command authority. Powerful men pause all the time because no one would dare interrupt them. Women who are incredibly powerful often develop speech patterns that are considered more traditionally male, such as speaking slower and pausing more. If you see an interview with Oprah, or Maya Angelou, or Hillary Clinton, they own their silences! Look back on earlier footage of Oprah. You'll see that she utilized silence less. As she moved from Oprah, just another talk show host, to *the* Oprah, she gained power and in turn used silence more often and effectively.

Unfortunately, for many of us, silence is one of the most difficult communication tools to wield. The reason is twofold.

Firstly, we often develop compensatory strategies to deal with interruptions that are counterproductive to claiming space. We employ what I call filler words and sounds, things such as "ah," "er," "but," and "you know," in order to fill space, thus preemptively stopping interruptions. Unfortunately, speaking without utilizing silence is a disempowered speech pattern. Never pausing, or taking a "beat" as we say in the acting world, makes you look more nervous and less assured.

Secondly, silence is one hell of a power move. A woman who knows how to use silence is a woman in control of her communication. She is a space claimer who is signaling with her speech patterns, in no uncertain terms, that she has the right to speak without interruption and claim space without apology. Unfortunately, so many of us have been trained that we don't have the right to pause when we are making a point. We quite literally don't take enough time even to breathe—a baseline requirement for healthy sound production, and living! Instead, we rattle off our opinions quickly while taking quick, shallow breaths. In doing so, we are telegraphing the following: "I know you might interrupt me, but don't worry, there will be no consequences, and maybe I don't have the right to this opinion, so, um, yeah, I won't take a lot of your important time, you know, making this point, so it's OK if you don't take me too seriously because I don't think I have the right to claim space with silence anyway."

And, oh yeah, besides filler words, we often use run-on sentences to pack a bunch of information into one uninterrupted idea.

As with cadence, avoiding silence has positive short-term outcomes. Primarily, we are not interrupted, nor are we accused of being too authoritative (read "bitchy"). Yet in the long run, our silence diminishes us. The cost of making ourselves small for another human is far worse than the short-term gain playing small affords.

Thankfully, you can learn to harness silence like Wonder Woman uses her lasso and claim space with your silence!

The Mechanics

There are only a handful of speech tools that can be used "offensively" or "defensively." Offensive techniques are used to make a point. Defensive tools are used to save you when you're in trouble. Most speech techniques are best used for one or the other. Silences can be used both offensively or defensively, which is why I love them!

OFFENSIVE SILENCE: I HAVE A POINT TO MAKE, AND YOU WILL HEAR ME

Non-actors use pausing mindfully for comedic or dramatic effect all the time. Whether you're giving a speech or talking with friends, you need to learn to identify when a dramatic pause would be in order. Some people do this intuitively, yet many struggle with knowing where to pause. The reality is, there is no wrong place to offensively pause, as long as you own that pause. There are, however, some tried-and-true places where you can be pretty confident about pausing:

✳ When you're making a point, pause before or after.

✳ Pause after a short sentence and before a long one.

- Don't say: No, I don't think that Tom should get a raise over me.

- *Do* say: No. [beat] I don't think Tom should get a raise over me.

Once you have identified the moment, go for it. Trust your decision and pause without apologetic body language!

1. **Take a beat and don't apologize.** After you have identified the moment, force yourself to pause far longer than you think. If you are not used to silence, what you think is way too long a pause is probably just right. When I teach silence in workshops, I often tell folks to pause and count to five slowly. Afterward I ask if the pause felt too long. They almost always say yes. Then I ask the other participants what they thought. Universally, they say no. It was powerful and it was perfect. Counting slowly for three to five seconds is usually enough to make a point.

2. **Make eye contact and don't look away.** This is critical. Look away while you're offensively pausing, and the probability of you being interrupted skyrockets. You also give away your power. Be sure to make direct eye contact with the person you're speaking to. If you're in front of an audience, still your body and look at the audience, blinking as little as you possibly can and moving your head minimally.

   If you are having trouble maintaining eye contact, at the very least be careful to never turn your head away, and *never* look toward the floor.

DEFENSIVE SILENCE: BUY TIME SO THAT YOU CAN REGROUP

The best way to use silence defensively is by coupling it with your body.

1. **Gain awareness and predict disaster.** Have you ever seen someone who is rambling on, making no sense? You can tell they aren't sure what to say, and it starts to look like a slow-motion train wreck. Have you ever seen someone at a loss for words, looking completely humiliated? Have these things happened to you? I would guess they have, as they happen to all of us. A great space claimer knows how to avoid this. It's not that they always know what to say. They simply know how to claim space with silence in order to regroup and come back to the conversation stronger.

   The first step is to gain an awareness of when you're headed for disaster. Most of us don't realize this until it's way too late. Learn moments when a break with pausing is in order. Start noticing that feeling in your gut when you're going off the rails. This will allow you to pause well before it's too late and you're already on the slow-moving train crashing into communication oblivion. Most of us ignore the signs, thinking that if we soldier on it will get better. It rarely does. It gets worse. Thankfully (yes, thankfully!), negative feelings have a myriad of very specific, and different, unpleasant flavors. Learn what "Oh crap, I'm going off the rails" feels like, and you will predict, and avert, disaster before it happens.

2. **Use your body and look pensive.** Decide how you are going to stop talking. There are several ways to manage the logistics of cutting yourself off when you're headed for disaster. The best way is to use your body. American cultural expectations are such that we don't comment on anything that has to do with people's bodies. In fact, in professional settings we are supposed to pretend we don't *have* bodies, and others don't as well! This is why when people do things to take care of their

bodies, we are supposed to pretend we don't notice. We look away or stare forward, as if time has stood still. You can use this to your advantage!

If you're sitting, whether in a meeting or hanging out in a group socially, adjust your body—for example, you can uncross and recross your legs. Hydrating also often works, as long as you hydrate midsentence.

Silence techniques for standing work mostly during presentations, specifically if you are not behind a podium but instead walking around. In this case, just walk into a stop. When people walk into a stop, it is socially acceptable to pause during the moment before they walk into the stop, for a few moments after they have stopped, and when they exit the stop. The important thing is to look like you are seriously engaged in what you're saying and not even a little apologetic.

Unlike with offensive silence, you don't need to maintain eye contact and look straight forward when using defensive silence. Human beings don't think looking forward. We look to the upper right and left, and lower right and left. Look in any of these directions, while moving your body, and you'll look pensive, not insecure. Just be sure to maintain strong eye contact again when you resume talking.

3. **Resume talking.** When you resume talking, it's absolutely critical you do so with confidence and without uttering a word of apology. I quote my formative acting teacher Phil Gushee to my students all the time. He often said, "Don't be embarrassed about how you got to a certain emotion. It's not printed in the program notes!" The same applies here. Whether you were internally panicking or cool as a cucumber, what you were feeling during the pause is no one's business but yours. Own your silence like a boss and reenter the conversation like a boss. You will look thoughtful and powerful, not scared and unconfident. Practice silence often, even when you don't need to take a beat. The more you do it, the more comfortable you will get with it and the more powerful your speaking will become!

I love the power of what our voices can do. Recently after a talk, I was on the receiving end of that power. I was in the bathroom, washing my hands, thinking about how I was cutting my flight home close and absolutely could not run the risk of turning my flight into an Olympic dash! As I was thinking and washing my hands, a pretty young woman with blazing red curly hair and a loud green blazer popped up out of her stall, then sidled up to the sink next to mine. Flashing me a toothy grin, she said a bit too loudly, "I lovvvvved your talk!"

"Thank you!" I responded politely. I usually love talking to people, but I had a flight to catch, and there was no way I'd be running in my yummy but highly impractical shoes.

The young woman smiled at me again, leaned in, and said, "I just have one question."

I would not get to the airport late! I would not!

Then she dropped her volume down to barely a whisper, "Would it be OK if I took just a few minutes of your time? It's a really quick question."

The power of her voice kept me from leaving the ladies' bathroom for a very long time. Learn to harness your voice, but try to use your newfound powers for good. Don't trap unwitting speakers in bathrooms! (For the record I did catch my flight, but my throbbing feet were not at all happy.)

BODY LANGUAGE

Posture matters. Voice matters. Words matter. But behavior matters more. Much more . . . And I'm about to blow your mind.

This chapter on body language will change the way you move your body in space, and therefore the way people respond to you, forever. Sound like bullshit? Understandable, but I challenge you to read on.

High/Low Behaviors—Power Tools for Wonder Women

Deborah Gruenfeld is a brilliant professor at Stanford University's Michelle R. Clayman Institute for Gender Research on Voice & Influence. She has, quite simply, cracked the code of how physicality and power dynamics intersect.[1] Once you understand and master Gruenfeld's body language techniques, you'll walk into high-stakes situations confident in your body, fully able to read the room, and with a deep understanding of power. You'll know exactly how to maintain it, grab it, and relinquish it.

To begin with, she starts with the following premise, one I couldn't agree with more: people don't listen to *what* we say. Indeed, her research shows that while only 7 percent of how we respond to people comes from hearing *what* words people say, 93 percent comes from *how* those words are delivered.

My clients tend to spend a great deal of time practicing the *what* while wholly ignoring the *how*. Indeed, most of us do.

What words will we say when we . . .

✳ Pitch an idea?

✳ Talk to someone who hurt our feelings?

✳ Give our speech?

✳ Ask a romantic interest on a date?

We need to stop focusing most of our efforts on the *least* important part of our communication—*what* we say. Instead, we need to work on what people actually pay attention to—*how* we say it.

Gruenfeld divides the how of body language as it relates to power into two distinct categories: high-playing behaviors and low-playing behaviors.

High-playing behaviors look like the body language folks often telegraph when they are in the power position and want people to know it—think claiming space, but on steroids.

Low-playing behaviors look like the body language folks often telegraph when they are not in the power position and want people to know it—not just ceding space, but relinquishing it.

Interestingly, under the right circumstances the behaviors that compose each category are not bad or good. Don't make the mistake of thinking you should only "play high" or "play low" as a rule. The goal is simply to control your communication by identifying and using these behaviors when navigating power dynamics.

High-Playing Behaviors

How to scare the crap out of someone even if your words sound really nice.

* **Take up space with your body!** On an airplane or in a movie theater? Manspread! Unapologetically claim both of your armrests!

* **Ignore people's "bubbles"—push into their space!** Personal bubbles? What personal bubbles? My bubble is *my* bubble, and *your* bubble is *my* bubble! I'm a little too close to you while we talk? You're welcome. (And if you don't like how close I am, *you* can step back.)

* **Speak in complete sentences, whether long or short.** You understand exactly what I mean. Don't ramble on. Don't use fragmented sentences. That's not powerful. Watch people who are powerful. Their sentences usually have a clear beginning, middle, and end. I find short sentences to be more powerful than long ones. Take control. Say less.

* **Stare at folks, keep your head absolutely still, try not to blink, and never, ever look away.** If you're having trouble imagining what this looks like, think back to being a recalcitrant senior in high school. If you weren't as rebellious as I, you'll have to use your imagination.

    Now remember, in this order . . .

    > Sneaking out of your house and then
    >
    > going to a party and then
    >
    > drinking one too many beers and then
    >
    > sneaking back into your house and then
    >
    > tiptoeing toward the kitchen to get some water and sal-tines because you heard this will mitigate hangovers and then
    >
    > rounding the corner to the kitchen only to find . . .

both your dad and your stepmother standing there, staring at you! Noooooo!

"Where have you been?" That's all your stepmom says.

And you almost *die* out of sheer terror!

Yes, *what* she said wasn't scary, but *how* she said her words, and *how* your dad was looking at you, made you want to *die*! Your parents' heads were as still as statues. They were barely blinking. They never broke eye contact. *And that's why they scared the crap right out of you.* (As a parent I have to say you shouldn't sneak out of the house. Do as I say, not as I did.)

✳ **When someone is talking to you, don't look at them.** Ever present an idea to someone and they didn't even take the time to look at you? Whether consciously or unconsciously, they did that to make you feel small. *Not looking at someone when they talk to you is a serious power move.* Remember when you ran into the living room as a kid and said, "Mommy! Mommy! Look at my picture!" Your mom glanced over for a split second, then looked back at her work while saying, "That's great, honey." Remember that? That was a serious power move. Mom was saying, "I'm in charge. I can't look at this now." Maybe that's why you were so mad when your first boss did the same thing to you after you finished a big project: "That's great. Leave it on my desk." It felt just like when you tried to show your mom those damn pictures. In both situations you intuitively understood that no matter how dismissed you felt, you were not in charge and would have to come back later to get real feedback. They had closed the subject. You had been power played.

✳ **Interrupt, without apology, before you know what you're going to say.** I don't know about you, but I *love it* when I'm in a meeting, in the middle of a sentence, my fully formed thought flowing out of my mouth smooth as butter, and a man (it is usually a man) interrupts me with this: "Well, I . . ." And then I have to wait, in silence, until said man thinks, a lot, before finishing his sentence. All the while I'm thinking, "Well, damn, I had an end to my sentence ready to go, and now I have to sit here politely while this powerful man gets to interrupt me before he knows what he's going to say? Really?"

Ladies, you know exactly what I'm talking about. Make no mistake. That's a power move.

Low-Playing Behaviors

There really are times you should play small.

* **Don't be a ballerina.** Jerk your hands around rather than moving in a more fluid, graceful way. You may have found yourself doing this while very nervously trying to make a point.

* **When talking with your hands, keep them close to your face.** Your hands don't need to move; resting your hand on your chin while talking accomplishes the same thing. I do this a lot when I'm mentoring someone who's nervous. I make myself a little small to help them feel more relaxed.

* **Give up your space—literally give it away.** This is the opposite of claiming space. Relinquish those armrests! Make sure your arms are glued to your sides, especially if you must call attention to yourself.

* **Lean forward, and if you want to go really low, Gruenfeld talks about pointing your toes together.** While some low-playing behaviors are great in certain contexts, I don't ever recommend this one. It feels childlike, diminishing, and generally awful. Indeed, I can't think of a time it would make sense to adopt this posture. Be sure to watch for this in people you're mentoring. If you see this, there is a trust gap going on. Your body has said to your mentee, "Bow down to me!" If this is happening, I'm guessing you are playing too high. Unless your mentee is being a huge jerk and you meant to scare them into their place, play a bit lower.

* **Speak in incomplete sentences.** Like, I have . . . you know . . . I have an idea . . . and, well, I'm wondering if maybe you, if you have a . . . if you're not free to hear my idea, I mean . . . that's totally OK. I mean, do you know what I mean? I can come back . . . if that's better . . .

* **Overtalk, often in run-on sentences.** This is mine, not Gruenfeld's, but it's definitely low. You know what I mean, don't you? I mean if you don't, that's totally, totally, *totally* fine, and if you don't agree, I get it because it's really up for debate, but I'm just saying this in case you're interested.

* **If you're talking to a high-status person, don't make a lot of eye contact.** If someone intimidated by you has pitched you an idea, you know exactly what this looks like. They state their opinion while looking away from you often and glancing down a lot. When they do look at you, it's to check in to see if you approve.

* **When a high-status person talks to you, show some respect— glue your eyes to theirs.** Unless you're *really* aware of your body, you will predictably do this, without knowing it, when someone is high playing you. I demonstrate high behavior during my talks on an unsuspecting audience member. Every time it's almost as if I've put a spell on them. They stare at me like a deer caught in the headlights, with a look of submissive discomfort. (I know this sounds mean, but I promise I low play them later, and we share a good laugh afterward.)

* **Smile. Constantly.** Gruenfeld calls constant smiling the "badge of appeasement," heretofore referred to as the BOA. Creepy. Low-status folks use the BOA to make sure the high-status person is comfortable. When I work with leaders, they will often walk me through the building to their corner office. As we walk, once in a great while everyone we see, and I mean everyone, greets us with huge, enthusiastic perma-smiles plastered on their faces. After we reach the corner office and shut the door, the boss invariably says something like this,

"Did you see how they were all smiling? They all *love* me!" I respond with, "Nope. They're deeply afraid of you." (Actually, I'm more delicate than that. But I've always wanted to say that just to see what happens.)

To understand and eventually master these behaviors, you need to practice. Here's how:

1. Get together with a girlfriend, or even better, a group of girlfriends.

2. Look over these behaviors—put them in front of you so you remember them.

3. Set a timer to go off every two minutes.

4. Talk to each other, and every time the timer goes off, switch from high to low behaviors. (Do *not* tell each other which you will be using first.)

5. Do this for at least six minutes.

6. Have your minds blown.

7. Process how much your minds were blown over a bottle of wine.

8. After your night of communication fun and wine, take the skills out of your house and practice them in low-stakes situations.

9. Once you're sure you can nail them in low-stakes situations, start bringing them into high-stakes situations.

10. Blow your mind repeatedly as you consistently shift interactions at work.

Eliza, the CEO Slayer

My favorite client story ever is about high- and low-playing behaviors. It illustrates when you should play high, how to do it, and what happens when you adopt Gruenfeld's strategies, wielding those skills like Wonder Woman's lasso.

But before we dive in, you need to know when to play high. Keep these in mind as you read the story I'm about to share.

Play high when you need to

* Grab status and power.

* Maintain status and power.

* Scare the living crap out of someone and make sure they never mess with you again. (I added this one. The top two are Gruenfeld's.)

Years ago, Bob, a powerful founder and CEO of a big company, asked me to come to him for some private coaching. Bob lived in an opulent yet rustic home on an island . . . that he owned. To be clear, he owned both the home *and* the island.

If you ever get filthy rich, I highly recommend buying an island.

Apparently when you're this rich, beyond buying an island, you can also throw your money around in all kinds of other fun and unexpected ways. In Bob's case, he and his fellow zillionaires liked to spend their spare time competing in an annual public speaking competition. I'm not clear on all the details, but this competition involved putting money into a pot, then getting together and presenting short speeches to each other. Whoever won "best speech" was awarded a cute little prize, in the form of a cool $1 million.

Like many CEOs, Bob was incredibly competitive and hated to lose. The previous year he had his butt handed to him, so that year he decided to work with me as his speech coach. Bob didn't want to travel or work remotely, and thus I was summoned to his island to help him rewrite and present his speech.

Once you were on the island, none of the doors to the houses were locked. Bob told me just to come to the main house, announce myself, and walk right in. I did. After walking through what, as a parent, I considered a dream mudroom, I rounded the corner and stepped into a tastefully decorated open kitchen. It had a huge counter for hosting their many friends, with a big window so we all had a great view of Bob's island.

Bob was in the kitchen, pacing, and he was on the phone. Actually, that sounds like he was *talking* on the phone. He was not. Bob was just doing something on the phone. Could have been Facebook, but I really don't know what he was doing. I only know it was an activity he could have stopped doing when I greeted him. But he didn't.

"Hi!" I said, full of enthusiasm.

Bob simply nodded, not at me but to his phone, and mumbled, "Glad you're here. Check your email. We sent you info on the cottage you'll be staying in and how to find it. See you soon."

Now, before Gruenfeld, I would have felt crappy and demeaned but would not have understood exactly why. I also wouldn't have known how to address the situation. Post Gruenfeld, I knew the body language power code. Bob not looking at me was a total power move—he was establishing who the boss was, and he wanted me to go along with the fact that it was him.

This just wouldn't do. Not at all. I wasn't going to spend a weekend working with a guy who had decided there was a pecking order and he was on top. Besides disliking how I felt about this, I also knew if I was going to effectively coach Bob, we needed to be equals. Once power dynamics are established, it becomes much harder to reboot them. It was time to break out Gruenfeld!

Even today, in the year 2020, in most work and personal situations it's the unspoken job of the women to keep the men comfortable in communication exchanges. If you don't believe me, watch men and women communicate. When there's an awkward moment, or a tense moment, who usually smooths it? Unless the woman is more powerful than the man, I will put my money on the woman, every time. In this case, keeping things running smoothly would have involved me cheerfully saying, with great warmth, "Great! I got the email! I'll go figure out which house I'm staying in and catch up with you later!"

As a powerful man, Bob was rarely if ever expected to fill awkward silences with cheerful chatter. That's the job of the less powerful interacting with him. Bob was the boss man at work, and his friend group treated him like the rock star boss man he was at work even during their personal time together. So, the first step to my resetting our power dynamic involved me disrupting expectations that Bob would be taken care of by yours truly.

I did this by purposefully and completely dropping the communication ball. Interrupting power moves by men is still emotionally challenging for me. It goes against years of training. Thankfully, I've mastered the art of being scared as hell but doing what I needed to do anyway. In this case what I needed to do was *not do a damn thing*. I needed to shut up. So I did. I didn't respond to Bob. Not a word. Not a sound. Thankfully and predictably, my Jedi mind trick worked.

Bob was fully startled by my silence, immediately turning his head to look at me.

The plan was working—that was win number 1!

Once Bob's surprised and confused eyes were locked onto mine, I said these banal words, "Great. I got the email. I'll go figure out which house I'm staying in and catch up with you later." In hindsight, what happened next was pretty hilarious. It was as if water had been poured over his head!

Bob almost dropped his phone, gave me his full attention, offered me a huge BOA—that's badge of appeasement, lest you forgot—smiled, and walked toward me, thrusting out his hand to shake mine: "Great! Great! Great! I look forward to working with you as well!" And with that, Bob's communication boot was heretofore removed from my proverbial neck!

So, what happened? How did I get this super-rich CEO who owned an island to respond to me like a man who suspected I might conjure lightning?

Let's look again at the words I said:

"Great. I got the email. I'll go figure out which house I'm staying in and catch up with you later."

Note that *what I said* doesn't read like a power play. But remember, words don't matter. It's all about how I said it, and how I said it was a power play.

I shifted the dynamic not by using different words but by dropping the enthusiasm in my voice. I telegraphed this by leaving out the exclamation points the second time. I also put my body in full Gruenfeld power-grab battle mode. As I said those words, *I adopted all the high-playing behaviors I could think of.* I didn't move my head. I didn't blink. I leaned on the handle of my suitcase, expanding my body as much as I could. I didn't scowl, but I did erase any hint of a smile. In short, I high played Bob, fully, and it worked like a charm.

For the rest of the weekend, Bob and I got along just fine. This would never have been possible had Bob established, and kept, his dominance. It would have been close to impossible for me to coach Bob, as he would not have respected my authority.

Sometimes, Go Small

There are times you should make yourself small. I know this goes against everything you've read in this book thus far. Don't panic.

After hearing my victorious Bob story, you may be wondering why the hell women should ever play low. Good question. In the immortal words of Mr. T, "I'm so tough and so bad, I can be humble and lift another guy up." (For those who are too young to remember Mr. T, watch *The A Team*. It may seem somewhat offensive now, but Mr. T will forever be cool.)

Beyond Mr. T . . . Gruenfeld recommends that you should specifically play low in the following situations:

* To show people you know your status is lower
* To raise up someone else's status and power
* To help people feel comfortable around you
* To convince people you are far less scary than they think you are

I added the final one. If you are the sort of person that is regularly told you are "intimidating," learning how to strategically play low can help people feel more comfortable and more open around you.

Playing low may sound like it's a dangerously effective way to diminish yourself. It is, but only when used at the wrong time. If I had played low with Bob, things would not have worked out well. That said, it is just as empowering to play low in some cases as it is to play high. *Indeed, playing low is like body language empathy— it helps people feel listened to, safe, and connected to you.*

Here are a few situations where playing low is the right thing to do. To be clear, these are from me, not Gruenfeld.

WHEN YOU MEET A POWERFUL PERSON AND WANT TO SHOW YOUR RESPECT

Years ago, when I was an insecure college student at the University of Colorado Boulder, I had the opportunity to meet Dr. Maya Angelou, who just happened to be my hero. Her books had literally helped me survive my less-than-optimal childhood, making me feel less isolated and helping develop my unshakable belief in the power of love.

Dr. Angelou had come to our campus to give a talk, and there was a reception afterward that I was invited to. I remember distinctly one interchange with a young woman who approached her. The young woman walked over to Dr. Angelou and immediately began stumbling over her words, rambling on anxiously about how Dr. Angelou was her hero, and what she meant to her, and she just couldn't explain in words what meeting her meant, and, and, and . . . Dr. Angelou, smiling at her, finally interrupted this young woman's spiraling torrent of words mid-sentence. "Kiss me," she said, leaning her goddess-like six-foot frame over the stunned, much shorter young woman like the benevolent Queen Angelou she was. Then she pointed to her cheek, "Right here."

The young woman hesitated for a moment, and then kissed Dr. Angelou on the cheek, looking as if she might burst into tears with joy. "Thank you," Dr. Angelou said, in her sincere and almost otherworldly way, putting her hand majestically on the young woman's shoulder. She then quietly said something close to the young woman's ear, something that clearly rocked her world, turned away, and continued to mingle. The young woman stood there, dumbstruck, and on cloud nine.

In this scenario, what Dr. Maya Angelou did with her body was the power move. Besides smiling, which softened her body language just a bit, she played high. She maintained direct eye contact. She barely moved her head. She moved into the young woman's bubble, touching her shoulder and whispering in her ear. And it was all just *fine*! Indeed, it was appreciated. Why? Because Dr. Angelou was in the position of respect. She was allowed to do that! Indeed, Dr. Angelou intuitively understood this young woman saw her as an all-powerful figure, so she let her entire powerful self fly, living up to the young woman's lionized version of her.

On the other hand, that young woman did the right thing by playing low. If she had moved her body in space similarly to Dr. Angelou, she would have appeared borderline insane. By playing low, she showed Dr. Angelou she understood she was talking to a queen, and respected her queen-like status. Both players understood the power dynamic and played their parts. No one was diminished by it.

Sometimes you want to show you respect someone's status by playing low. Sometimes you want to wow people by playing high. I would never, ever walk up to Lizzo and put my hand on her shoulder. If, however, she put her hand on my shoulder when meeting me, I would be thrilled!

WHEN YOU MENTOR OR LEAD THOSE WITH LESS POWER OR PRIVILEGE

I'm a Cook House Fellow at Cornell and spend a good deal of time mentoring undergraduate young women of color. For many reasons, there is a huge power differential, with me in the more powerful position.

* They are students of color. I'm White.

* They are younger; I'm older.

* They are students; I'm established in my career.

* We meet on my "home turf," my kitchen, so they are guests.

It would be counterproductive and possibly damaging for me to play completely high with these young women. Even Dr. Angelou didn't do that, and she was a goddess temporarily walking amongst us humans on Earth. I would never sit in my kitchen with my mentees, head frozen, eyes locked on them with zero sign of a smile, and say, "So, how are you? Tell me everything." They wouldn't tell me a thing because my high-playing behaviors would be absolutely terrifying, not to mention an obnoxious power play. The more power and privilege you have in relation to the person you are talking to, the less appropriate it is to play high, especially if they are playing low. When mentoring, I often smile, chin resting on my hands, and glance around a bit while asking for an update. I build trust and actively work to put people at ease. I play low.

WHEN YOU INTERSECT WITH SOMEONE WHO IS SCARED OF YOU

If, for whatever reason, you notice someone is terrified of you and won't open up to you, try playing low. You will find this shifts the dynamic immediately, and they instantly feel more comfortable with you. I often do this when dealing with gatekeepers, such as admins, front desk folks in hotels, or nurses. These competent folks are woefully undervalued by society, often treated badly, and power played on the daily. When intersecting with them, I choose to take the opposite orientation that society expects me to. I plaster on the BOA, and I adopt a few other low-playing behaviors. I signal, with my body, my truth: although society thinks they are beneath me in status, I absolutely do not. Invariably, I forge strong connections quickly with these folks, and they often become fierce allies. I can't tell you how many times I've been squeezed into someone's schedule or upgraded to a better room at a hotel without asking for an upgrade. You can forge important, and sometimes quite meaningful, relationships with folks just by refusing to play into society's power expectations. Try it. You'll get what you want a lot more often and, more importantly, create meaningful and unexpected connections with really wonderful people.

When to Go Low, When to Go High

If you're a bit confused about when to play high and when to play low, or just want to test your power dynamic prowess, please take the following little quiz.

Should you play high or low in the following circumstances?

1. Working with friendly but traumatized at-risk kids
   H/L

2. Shutting down a microaggression
   H/L

3. Talking to a police officer when pulled over
   H/L

4. Giving a keynote
   H/L

5. Meeting your new boss
   H/L

6. Disagreeing with your partner
   H/L

7. Pitching to a VC
   H/L

8. Talking with your teenager about a bad grade
   H/L

9. Running a meeting
   H/L

10. Communicating with your ex
   H/L

If you knew all the answers instantly, you get an F. Have no fear; this is normal! If you had to pause, really think about those answers, and then you concluded you would need more data before answering, well done! You're already developing a more nuanced approach to using these powerful tools. Congrats! You're outside of the bell curve! There are no right or wrong answers in that trick quiz. As in life, 1–10 are all fully dependent on the details and nuances of the situation.

Before diving in and using these behaviors, examine yourself and the players you will be intersecting with. Then think about the following:

* Your stakes and goals

* Players' stakes and goals

* Personality traits/demographics/cultures of players

* Power status among players

* Historic group and/or individual power dynamics

* Costs of making players uncomfortable

* Benefits of putting players at ease

* Kinds of high or low behaviors players typically use

Once you look at all of these factors, you can choose your high/low approach. In the end, 99 percent of the time you should probably choose a blend, rather than one or the other. It will take some trial, error, and practice, but you can and will master them.

Finally, in case you're wondering, Bob did not win the competition. He got second. At the time he insisted he should have won. From where I'm sitting, given the place his speech started before I arrived, Bob was a very lucky man. And Bob was a man who should really thank Deborah Gruenfeld because with the help of a few high-playing behaviors, our weekend was productive rather than a drawn-out *Clash of the Titans*–style power struggle. While I had hoped he would win, he survived his third-place finish and is still living happily on his island. Truth is, Bob really wouldn't have noticed that $1 million had it dropped into his bank account anyway.

Mirroring

Have you ever been in a meeting, or in a job interview, or on a date, and felt like you were slowly, ever so slowly, losing your authority . . . and you had no idea why the hell it was happening? While the reasons for this feeling can be multifactorial, one of my go-to questions for clients is this: How were they sitting and how were you sitting?

Most of the time the answer confirms my suspicion. My client was unconsciously ceding power with her body language.

Mirroring is a simple quick-and-dirty strategy you can easily implement in order to connect with people, increase your powers of persuasion, and level power dynamics.

What is mirroring? Mirroring is what it sounds like—positioning your body in such a way that your posture and body positioning mimics the person you're talking to.

Mirroring practice: grab a friend and try this.

1. Both of you sit facing each other, leaning in, with your forearms resting on your upper thighs and fingers interlaced. How do you feel? I'm guessing you both feel comfortable, engaged, maybe even a little conspiratorial.

2. Now, slouch way back in your chair while your friend continues to lean in. How do you both feel now? Your friend probably feels either aggressive or as if you are looking down on her. You probably feel attacked or superior. One thing is certain: you both don't feel good!

3. Now have your friend slouch way back in her chair. How do you both feel now? I'm guessing you feel similar to how you did in scenario 1, except more relaxed and casual.

4. Finally, have your friend stay back while you go to position 1, with your forearms resting on your upper thighs and fingers interlaced. In other words, flip scenario 2. I'm guessing the feelings are exactly like scenario 2, but in reverse. And yet again, neither of you feels good.

In a landmark 2010 Belgium study titled "Why Do I Like You When You Behave like Me? Neural Mechanisms Mediating Positive Consequences of Observing Someone Being Imitated," researchers found the following:

> Our results indicate that being imitated compared to not being imitated activates brain areas that have been associated with emotion and reward processing, namely medial orbitofrontal cortex/ventromedial prefrontal cortex (mOFC/vmPFC, GLM whole-brain contrast). Moreover mOFC/vmPFC shows higher effective connectivity with striatum and mid-posterior insula during being imitated compared to not being imitated.[2]

Here's what the scientists said, summarized like an actual human might have said it:

> Mirroring immediately puts you on par emotionally with people, rapidly building rapport.

Mirroring is one of the quickest and easiest skills to learn. It's a powerful tool in your communication arsenal, and the research backs this up.

Don't think mirroring can make that big a difference? An article on the website Science of People cited several studies that prove the mighty power of mirroring![3] The studies showed that when mirroring happened, waitresses gained higher tips and sales clerks achieved higher sales and more positive evaluations.

Mirroring Mechanics

Here's the key to mirroring: do it subtly. If the person you're talking to changes position, don't immediately mirror the change. You don't want to give away that you have secret persuasive superpowers! Instead, slowly move into the position of your counterpart, but don't mirror them completely—just echo their posture. For example, if you're asking for a raise from your boss and they are casually lounging way back in their chair, don't lounge quite as much. Lean back just a little. This will show deference while also indicating you're worthy of the raise. You're saying with your posture, "Hey boss, I'm your equal, I'm on your level, and therefore you should take me seriously when I ask for a raise."

Perhaps the most common question I'm asked in Q&A about landing jobs and mirroring is this: "Who should I mirror in a job interview if there is more than one person on the panel?" The answer is twofold:

1. **If everyone at the table is sitting in different postures** . . . then mirror the alpha (a.k.a. the boss). This will signify you are on par with the alpha and worthy of everyone's respect. It will also unconsciously build rapport with the alpha.

2. **If the alpha is sitting in one position and everyone else is sitting identically in another**, particularly if the alpha is casually leaning back and everyone else is ramrod straight . . . *do not* mirror the alpha. This scenario indicates the alpha has established dominance and a clear pecking order. Everyone else is expected to show they respect the alpha's status by not mirroring the boss lady's posture. She is the boss. They are the deputies. Period. Otherwise, you're saying, "Hey, I know everyone else thinks you're super powerful, but not *this* lady. I'm *just* as cool as you!"

Mirroring is a down and dirty way to build rapport and influence people. It can accelerate building connections with a new friend. It can help persuade when pitching to a VC. It makes you a better negotiator and it will help you land a job. Remember to do it, and this targeted tool will be a useful one in your ever-growing superhero communication bag of tricks.

Final Tips

Before you move on to the next part, some final advice about presenting like a space-claiming boss: if anything I said in this part really doesn't work for you, don't do it.

I've noticed that clients tend to feel bad if they can't master tools that just don't work for them or make them feel inadequate. On the flip side, they devalue the tools that play to their strengths and make them feel capable and empowered. My take on this is that throughout our lives people tell us again and again that who we are isn't enough. Eventually, we begin to see our strengths, which should empower us, as weaknesses.

Not all of these tools will work for every woman, and that's fine. We all have strengths and weaknesses. Try all the skills, but understand that some of the tools will play to your strengths more than others. Use those. They will help you claim space more, because they are playing to the strengths you have, and those strengths, if nurtured, are more than enough.

Posture, voice, body language. It might seem like a lot to learn, but remember this. When it comes to physicality and voice, the stages of learning go like this:

1. You don't know what you don't know.

2. You know what you don't know, but you can't do it.

3. You can do it, but only if you really think about it.

4. You can do it without thinking about it.

You probably started this part in stage 1. You are now, probably, in stage 2. Stage 2 is the *worst*, but have no fear! Just practice these skills, a lot. Before you know it, you will be in stage 3. Then, not too far from now, you'll realize you are forgetting to remind yourself to stand tall, project, or slow down. And yet you're using these tools anyway in persuasive and inspiring ways. In that moment you'll understand why people have been deferring to you a little more, interrupting a little less, and giving you one armrest without a fight. You have been claiming space, and people are taking notice. You are presenting like a boss.

PART 2

CLAIM SPACE COLLAB- ORATIVELY

Amplify Each Other!
Forge relationships that uplift you.

Behind every successful woman is a tribe of successful women who have her back.
—ANONYMOUS

I make my living talking in front of people. During the pandemic, about a week after New York went into quarantine, my business collapsed. There was simply no work. I was terrified, worried I would lose everything. Thankfully, I had the best insurance possible, and I don't mean the kind you pay for with money. My payments were made in caring, time, networking, and helping women however I could throughout my life. What I got from these payments was my network, and it was strong.

Keep a group disconnected and you disempower them. Create structures that encourage another group's strong professional and personal connections, and that group's power is augmented by orders of magnitude. Historically, systems have been in place specifically to encourage men to empower themselves by empowering each other, perpetuating and augmenting their power and influence. Country clubs, sports teams, informal get-togethers, after-work cocktails—all provided men ample opportunities for friendship and mentorship, forming the backbone of the old boy network.

It can be harder for women to support each other as men do—we face a multitude of barriers that keep us from forging connections in the same ways. We have less time. Childcare disproportionately falls on us. We have less access. Women are not in as many positions of power, so statistically we have fewer women who can connect with us. On top of this, men often exclude women, sometimes inadvertently and sometimes more purposefully. For example, they can't ask us into the men's locker room, but many a deal has been made there. They can ask us to go out for drinks with the "boys," but they often don't.

It's an uphill battle for women, which is why the extra effort we put in to take a page out of the men's playbook reaps huge rewards. #MeToo consisted only of women sharing their stories as a collective, and look at how we moved the needle! #MeToo must not be the destination; it must be the beginning, a launchpad for a new way of empowering through connection. If we support each other and claim space together, our voices and our power are amplified. This part will help you do just that by doing the following:

1. Teach you to eliminate the barriers that keep us from uniting and augmenting each other's voices.

2. Help you create a network that can accelerate your career.

3. Inspire you to construct a safety net that will create positive change for all of us.

I have cultivated an incredible group of women, both friends and in my work, over the last twenty years. Had I not called upon those women in my life to help me, I would have been sunk. Instead, I launched a remote online learning business and activated my network. Every woman I knew answered the call. They sent me business. They subscribed to my Patreon page. They talked up my services online. They talked to each other about how they could help and then followed through. They took my voice, and they amplified it.

In the end, I came out stronger than before the pandemic. I had been networking like a man my entire life. In many ways, it saved my life.

This part is about how we position ourselves to claim space together so we can amplify each other. It is a three-step process:

1. Claim space by knowing your worth.

2. Learn to spot prototypes of people who would make you small.

3. Forge connection.

We are all stronger when we have folks in our lives who will support us when we're down, applaud us when we're up, and stand side by side with us, demanding in a unified voice that we have the right to claim space together. It will offer concrete ways to build your network so that you are never really alone. Your sisters will be there, standing in solidarity with you, claiming space by your side . . . and straightening your crown.

The Scarcity Myth

All kinds of forces keep us from connection. One of the most powerful reasons that women stay disconnected is historically we have not had access to power and resources. This has created a collective feeling of scarcity for us. It can be hard to shake the feeling that there are not enough resources to go around, so you have to get what you can before it runs out. We've all been taught that there's only one "It Girl" at a time and that It Girl is us, or it's not.

Years ago, a client came to me for help. Sue was a middle-aged Asian woman working at a law firm. A rock star in her field, she was a partner, the only woman, and only woman of color, in her firm. Recently, June, a newly minted law school grad, had joined the firm as an associate. Sue came to me because June had been eviscerating her in meetings and just about every other place they intersected. Sue couldn't understand it and was looking for strategies on how to stop the dynamic. She was at the end of her rope and at that point was so furious with June she had begun preemptively cutting her down at every turn. Sue was feeling completely demoralized—she had pushed to hire June, excited to finally have a woman in her firm, and they seemed to be locked in a battle to the death!

When Sue was done telling her story, I paused for a moment and then said, "Is June Asian?"

Sue was flabbergasted. "Yes. How could you know that?"

"I think I know what's going on. You two are fighting for your spot on the bottom."

What is fighting for your spot on the bottom?

Historically, women have not had a seat at the tables of power. If a woman was there, there was only one of us, or just a few of us. A handful of White women. Only one Black, Asian, Latinx, or Indigenous woman. We were alone at the top and fighting to stay there, or fighting tooth and nail to move up the ladder. This historic memory, this feeling of scarcity, still remains.

Think of power as a triangle. At the top of this triangle is a mini-triangle. That triangle holds the power. Everyone below that top triangle has varying degrees of less power. The lower you go on the triangle, the less power you have. Historically that tiny top triangle has been reserved for men. Specifically, it has been reserved for White men.

When women somehow make it into that top triangle, we often feel, unconsciously, as if there is room for only one of us. And that's understandable. Often that has been the case. This is why women sometimes go after other women *and more so when that woman is in their demographic*. In Sue's case, June felt there was only room for one Asian woman, and that feeling of scarcity caused June to go on the attack.

Here's generally what happens:

1. The woman who's already in the power position unconsciously feels threatened by the up-and-comer.

2. The up-and-comer feels she'll never be able to move up if the woman already there at the top isn't pushed down.

Both of these responses, ironically, don't just hurt women in the moment. They also reinforce male power structures. While we are busy eviscerating each other, men are locking arms, going out for beers, hiring, collaborating, and promoting each other. And the cycle continues.

In Sue's case, I advised her to call June into her office and tell her how happy she was to have her working there, how she felt they had gotten off on the wrong foot, and that she would like to mentor June and support her however she could. This would help June to feel less threatened by Sue and probably put a stop to June's attacks.

I'd like to say that Sue jumped at the chance to do this. She did not. She was pretty pissed at June and highly skeptical that it would work. After the session I didn't hear from Sue for a month. Then she randomly called me out of the blue. Things had escalated since our session. June had been making Sue's life fully miserable, and Sue had regularly begun to respond in kind. Finally, out of desperation, after a painfully contentious staff meeting, Sue sucked up her rage and called June into her office. June walked in, looking particularly defensive. Sue launched into her prepared speech and then waited in silence. After a moment, June looked at her and then unloaded about just how hard it had been for her from day one, and how scared she was that if she made one false move she'd blow it. They ended up talking for an hour about their mutual experiences. They didn't leave as friends, but they left as allies.

Things got markedly better after that. Today the two are regular collaborators. Together they have helped each other ascend in the firm and successfully advocated to hire more women. They claim space together, and they are augmenting the hell out of each other.

There are other reasons why women are disconnected, besides fighting for our spot on the bottom. Historically, working-class women simply do not have the energy or time to network and sometimes even to socialize. Even if they do have time, the people they associate with often aren't powerful decision makers.

On the flip side, higher-income women often don't feel a sense of urgency to create their own professional networks. They do have access to economic resources, and this frees up their time to socialize. However, if they are in heterosexual relationships, they often have less power in the workplace than their husbands. The response to this is to derive much of their power through the men they are married to, which is highly problematic. When you rely on getting your power from another human being, you are beholden to that human being. That's not healthy for you, the person you are relying on, or the relationship.

The workplace is where decisions are made, and the people making them still look a lot like the decision makers in the TV show *Mad Men*. The majority of venture capitalist (VC) firms have no female partners. Not one. Collectively, women make up just 12 percent of the decision makers in American VC firms. For women of color, the numbers are markedly lower.[1]

In other words, White men collectively are augmenting each other, deciding what business ideas are birthed and which ideas never see the light of day in society. Thus, businesses are geared toward White men, run by White men. This is not some horrible conspiracy. White men are simply promoting businesses that speak to their experiences. This doesn't just happen in business. White men dominate space in every aspect of the workforce from academia to business to nonprofit organizations.

It's no different in politics—the Senate and the House, despite great strides, are still dominated by men. If men are connecting in the halls of power, what laws will be passed? Who will shape the priorities of our society?

Finally, leisure time. Women still do a disproportionate amount of childcare and housework. Study after study has shown that men have infinitely more leisure time. This has allowed them to spend more time networking with their colleagues at work but also just hanging out in their social circles. The more robust your social circle, the more powerful your professional network. Men have more time to join soccer leagues, go to country clubs, volunteer on boards . . . and in all of these spaces they are connecting with men from varied professions. And their connection gives them power. Claiming space isn't something that men have to think about doing; it is a part of their culture. It lies at the very foundation of their success.

Finally, we don't connect at work, even in the best of circumstances, because women often feel we have to do it on our own in order to prove we have a right to be in any given space. We feel that if we lean on other women we are somehow diminishing our own capabilities. The only male clients I have who regularly struggle with delegating are men of color. They too can feel that coworkers, subordinates, and bosses are looking at them as if they have to earn their spot at the table day after day. Every time they delegate, they feel they're admitting defeat. Women of color struggle with this most. The level of stressed-out women of color I work with who are doing their jobs in addition to the jobs of their subordinates is simply staggering. Men approach delegating without apology. Women approach delegating as if they're holding up a big sign that says, "I'm not capable." Delegating and collaborating builds connection. Doing it alone isolates.

A one-woman army is not going to shift the tide. It will not get women promoted more. It will not get women into the halls of power. It will not change society on a fundamental level.

The #MeToo movement was a profound reminder of the power we have as women when we connect and claim space together. #MeToo radically overhauled the expectations of how women should be treated in the workplace. It was a critical step. But it is not the only step. We must unite in the workplace, in the political arena, and in our personal lives. We must insist on leisure time. We must form radical women's knitting circles. We must join women-only volleyball leagues. We must meet for drinks after work. We must have women from varied circles over to our homes and insist we all trade business cards. I do this all the time—it's fun and a great way to network!

We must connect as if our very lives depended on it. Have you been hired by another woman? Felt the powerful solidarity of other women after saying #MeToo? Held your friend's hand as you gave birth? Been knocked flat on your face and cried with relief when your sisters lifted you up? Did you help a woman save her business during a global pandemic? Think back on your life and imagine what it would be like without the women in your life. If you have experienced any of this, you know that at some point in our lives, our very lives did depend on the connections we formed with other women. Now imagine you could multiply those experiences tenfold. You can. We can.

It's hard to have a space-claiming revolution with a one-woman army. So let's connect, claim space, and augment the hell out of each other. If enough of us do, when we have our fair share, we won't need to claim space anymore . . . because the space will finally be built by us, and for us. We will be welcomed to the door with a "Please, sister, come in! This space is for us."

KNOW YOUR WORTH

Many books on forming connections and mentoring focus primarily on the mechanics of network building. They completely ignore the critical first step. Step one for amplifying other women? Be comfortable amplifying yourself! You can't claim space with other women if you don't believe you can claim space for yourself.

"I know my worth, and I expect to be treated accordingly."

Think about meeting a woman who projects this energy. Do you want to spend time with her? I'm guessing you do. People who know their worth gravitate toward each other. So, the first step to connection is knowing your worth. This is the foundation for other skills, such as making demands, and will help you attract women into your life who claim space like bosses. Put two space-claiming women together and the amplification increases by orders of magnitude.

Know the Value You Bring

The first step to knowing your worth is understanding your value. Do this by flipping the script. The person who taught me how to do this was Tremayne, a Black man who mentored me when I first started working as a speaker. I had just been offered one of my first workshops and called up Tremayne in a panic. "Tremayne, I was just asked to tell these people what I charge for a workshop, and it's my first big workshop and I have *no idea* what to charge. So the workshop is about . . ." He cut me off, which in this case was justified, as he didn't need to know anything about what I was doing in order to advise me. Indeed, that would have clouded the issue. He wanted to teach me to fish, and knowing anything about what I was doing would have tempted him to give me the answer rather than help me find it myself.

"Eliza," he chuckled, "you don't need to tell me any more. You know what you should charge."

"No, I really don't."

What he said next is still burned into my brain.

"Well," he said, "whenever I'm unsure what to charge, here's what I do. I sit down. I close my eyes. And I think to myself, 'What would I charge if I were a White man?' And that's what I charge. It's usually double what I planned. You should try it."

I thanked him, got off the phone, and did the exercise. Tremayne was spot on. It was about double what I had been thinking of charging. Most White men are trained to know their worth, and that's a good thing! We should as well. If you struggle with this, use Tremayne's handy "What would a White man charge?" trick! Works like a charm!

Indeed, this concept can be applied in a myriad of ways. If you're collaborating on a project and you're finding that you're undervaluing your contribution, flip the script. If the man on the project were doing the same level of work you are, would you be giving him credit? The first step to taking credit is knowing what value you bring to the table.

This concept also works for relationships. If you find yourself giving more than your partner, flip the script. Would he tolerate this inequity from you? If not, it is fully within your rights to take credit for what you're doing and demand things change. This brings me to my final point about knowing your worth.

Make Demands

Once you decide what your value is, then you can determine what to ask for and make a demand. Sometimes when women make demands we face all kinds of pushback—pushback that I tackle later in this book. That said, most of the time when you advocate for yourself rather than remaining silent, you will feel better regardless of the outcome.

In the immortal words of Audre Lorde, "your silence will not protect you." Being silent about the things that matter to you slowly chips away at your ability to claim space. So speak up whenever you can safely. The more you do it, the more used to it you will become. You will become better at it, rise higher, and be better positioned to claim space with other women and raise them up.

When making demands, it's important to do it in the way that feels powerful and appropriate for you, and that you state your demand confidently, firmly, and without apology.

When it comes to being paid, don't lower your price. Ask for that White guy number. If you are collaborating, insist you be given credit for your disproportionate contributions. Or, if you aren't happy doing an unfair share, insist others step up. This can be challenging because history has taught us that women who ask without apology can be punished with unfortunate labels (see part 3, chapter 8) or painful pushback (see most of parts 4 and 5!). You have two choices.

1. **Make a demand without apology.** This is admirable, but it doesn't always work. The world doesn't always respond favorably to women who claim space. If you are in a position to deal with an outcome that is negative, I always recommend staying in your full power when you can. When you can, however, is the operative phrase. It's not always possible. Assess the situation carefully, and be sure you are ready for fallout before taking this approach. Of course, if every woman stopped making herself small, the world would have no choice but to get used to powerful women, but sometimes this just isn't possible.

2. **Soften your delivery.** Review part 1, chapter 3 on high and low behaviors. If you are willing to compromise, you may need to play just a tiny bit low—for example, employing a smile—to accomplish this. I hate advising women to smile. Indeed, it puts a horrible pit in my stomach. But I also understand that's a privileged perspective. For example, if you are a Black woman with a White boss in a predominantly unsupportive White male environment, and you have three kids counting on you getting a raise, lofty principles sometimes must take a back seat. Don't beat yourself up for doing what you need to do now. Eventually, you will be in a position to make demands with your full powerful self on display. You are doing what you need to do, and that's something to be proud of in a world where the odds are stacked against you.

If you are in a relationship and you realize you're not getting credit for your contributions to the partnership, it's time to point that out to your partner. But remember, pointing it out is not the end point. The next step is making sure that the situation is fair. They need to do more, or you can go on strike and do less! Let those dishes sit on the counter. Use paper plates if you have to.

You can't claim space for yourself if you are making yourself small, and as long as you are small, you can't raise up other women.

Own Compliments and Brag!

You can do this without sounding like an asshole. I'll show you how!

Once you know your worth and have made demands, claim even more space! Many women are terribly uncomfortable with this. Good little girls are demure, quiet, and self-effacing. Good little girls deflect compliments and don't brag. But you can't claim space if you are afraid to own and amplify your best qualities.

A few years ago, while still in high school, my daughter Ella modeled for me what a space-claiming woman should do. She walked downstairs, and I said to her, "Oh *Ella*, you look so beautiful today! You're such a beautiful young woman." She looked me right in the eyes, with no hint of "Who *me*? Noooooo!" Then, without missing a beat, she confidently said, "Thank you!" Somehow, I was taken aback. My response would have been to take the compliment but then insult myself in some way. Many women know this drill: "Thank you, but I hate my hair today" or "Thank you, but I wish I had your nose!" My daughter did none of this. With a simple "Thank you!" she turned that expectation right on its head.

"Ella!" I said. "I love that you own that!"

"Well," she said, "women are taught not to take compliments. Men don't do that. They own their good qualities; they don't apologize for them. So now, when someone says something nice to me, I just say, 'Thank you!' It's getting easier and easier."

What Ella did is the foundation of bragging. Owning what we are good at without apology. Practice being like Ella! Take compliments with confidence!

BUT ENOUGH ABOUT YOU . . .

You know which group of people does the best in job interviews? People with narcissistic personality disorder.[1] Why? They *love* to brag about themselves! "*Me* is so happy to tell you all about *me* because *me* loves *me* sooooo very much!"

Bragging well is a powerful way to let people know your good qualities—and build social capital. She who has a lot of social capital has a much easier time claiming space for herself and other women.

Listen closely the next time you're in a group. I will bet that the most successful braggers are also the most successful people with the biggest networks. Bragging helps you land jobs, nail Q&As, pitch to clients, and of course, network better. The benefits of bragging well are pretty much endless.

Most adept braggers enjoy bragging, and it comes naturally to them. Thankfully, even if you hate bragging, or lack an intuitive sense of how to do it, with direct instruction you too can learn the art of bragging like a champ.

BRAG LIKE A CHAMP EVEN IF YOU AREN'T A NARCISSIST

Let's start with an acronym: HSBH. This stands for the different parts of what I call the brag sandwich: humility—shameless brag—humility.

HSBH is actually not completely representative of the sandwich. More accurately, the sandwich is humility and hard work—shameless brag—humility and hard work. I shortened it to HSBH because HHWSBHHW was a bit harder to remember.

When talking about your accomplishments, use HSBH:

1. **Humility.** Begin your brag by talking about how thankful you are, or acknowledge the struggle you had to go through to get to where you are now.

2. **Shameless Brag.** Now that you have buffered your brag, insert the content you want to brag about.

3. **Humility.** End your brag by saying once again how thankful you are, or by acknowledging your hard road to success. I suggest rotating. If you started with gratitude, end with hard work. If you started with hard work, throw in some gratitude at the end. Just be sure you are being authentic. Never, ever lie, pretending to feel gratitude if you don't feel it. It's dishonest, and it will probably backfire. This technique is just a reminder to share your true gratitude and hard work, not an invitation to lie.

Here's an example. When asked how my business is going, I could say this:

> It's going really well, and I'm successful. I mean, I go all over the world giving talks!

You kind of don't like me, do you? I don't blame you!

Now I shall insert this in the brag sandwich. I have underlined the key words that get me off the hook for my shameless brag, and the bolded text is my original response.

I'm so filled with <u>gratitude</u>. **It's going really well, and I'm successful. I mean, I go all over the world giving talks!** It <u>hasn't been easy getting here</u>, and I have so much to be <u>thankful</u> for.

You like me a lot more now, don't you?

WHY WE BRAG BADLY, AND WHEN WE SHOULDN'T BRAG

Most people don't resent the triumphs of others. Resentment isn't an outgrowth of jealousy; it comes from the feeling that someone lacks humility or thankfulness. Bragging without the sandwich sounds like "I take my success for granted because I'm all kinds of awesome and I am so *owed* this!"

It can be very hard to claim space without flinching when saying "Thanks for the compliment," or "Look what I've done. I'm proud of myself. I did this." If advocating for yourself isn't enough motivation to brag, think about it this way: every time you brag, you increase your chances of advancing your career. Theoretically, you could be taking the spot of a narcissist who might be climbing the same ladder to success. Therefore, assuming you are not a narcissist, your bragging is not just helping yourself but helping us all. You will rise, while at the same time one less narcissist is out there making the world a little more miserable.

Slay Impostor Syndrome

Most people have a little voice that says, "Sure, we're succeeding, but we really don't know what the hell we're doing, and in short order, we will be exposed as the frauds that we are and all will be lost."

Let's kill that, shall we?

This exercise almost universally transforms clients in minutes. It works so well it's almost spooky.

I have three best friends in the world. Kim "Yoda/Morpheus" Munson-Burke, is one of them. Kim is a short woman with a wide smile and a brain like a clairvoyant. Kim works with people who have had severe trauma. She developed an incredibly effective strategy for them, which she has generously said I could share with you. It starts with the well-known psychological concept that we all have an inner child. Different experts have had various takes on this concept for years, from Carl Jung's "divine child" to John Bradshaw's "wounded inner child."[2]

As Kim tells it, when we act out, that's not our adult selves but our damaged younger selves making choices for us. That's where our "Why the *hell* did I do that?!" moments come from. Our kid selves have crawled onto our shoulders, are driving our ships, and are gleefully yelling "Wheeeee!" whilst making epically bad choices.

The exercise follows. I will be the first to admit it sounds weird, but it works. Please just try it.

1. Close your eyes and imagine you've entered the helm of a huge ship as "Adult You." Adult You knows if she were incompetent, she wouldn't be there. She is a grown woman who knows exactly how to do her job, and does it well. Adult You is a badass.

2. Now imagine Adult You is looking at the steering wheel of the ship. (You know, the kind that is a wheel with those spoke-like things all around it?) The person controlling the wheel is "Little You," you at the age you felt most vulnerable, insignificant, and incapable. This younger, often smaller, you is scared to death, and she's steering badly.

3. Walk over to Little You, and put your hand on her shoulder. Tell her this: "I know you're scared, and you should be, because you're not qualified to drive this ship."

4. Pause, look Little You in the eye (with care!), and then say, "But I do. I know how to pilot this ship. So, I need you to sit in that chair next to me because I'm going to drive now, and I know how. I know you're scared, and that's OK. But you are safe. I've got this."

5. Open your eyes. You should feel more rooted, calm, powerful, and competent. (Sounds weird, but don't you?)

Often when I talk about this in workshops or talks, several people immediately begin crying. We all know on an unconscious level when we have lost control of our ships; most of us just don't know how to wrestle the wheel back from the terrified, vulnerable little kid who still lives in us. Now, you do. Adult You can take the wheel. Adult You is strong, and she is capable.

SOME NUANCES ABOUT THIS EXERCISE

This is a powerful short-term fix for high-stakes situations, not a long-term fix. Unfortunately, only therapy can address this at its roots. For many of us, we didn't have just one time in our lives when things were hard; we had many. Start identifying how old you feel in different circumstances and what kinds of life events make you feel which age. If phrases like "Wow—she makes me feel like a little kid" or "I feel like an insecure teenager with him all over again!" pop into your head, you will know which version of you to envision moving from behind the wheel to the seat next to you on that ship. Be sure to practice this exercise *before* high-stakes situations. Don't wing it! This is a great exercise to use before interacting with antimentors, a category of person you really want to avoid that I'll talk about in the next section.

One of life's great ironies is that most of us are convinced, at one time or another, that we don't deserve to sit at the grown-ups' table. Confident grown-ups get to ask for what they want. Kids hope someone will give it to them one day. But we are not impostors, and we are not little kids. Every time we took a risk, raised up our sisters, overcame heartbreak, started a new career, stood unwavering in the face of injustice, or got up after falling flat on our faces, we grew. We became more fierce, more empathetic, more kind, more adult.

You're a competent, capable, badass woman who doesn't have to do it all to prove that.

You are a grown woman. Know your worth. Then watch as other women who know theirs journey into your life. Claim your space and sit down without apology at the grown-ups' table. You've earned it.

DISCONNECT FROM PEOPLE WHO WOULD MAKE YOU SMALL

Even when you feel really strong, there are people who can make you feel really small. If you let these people into your circle, or give them an important role in your life, it will be hard to ever feel like you deserve to be at the adults' table. There are the prototypes of those folks. Watch out for them. They will diminish your ability to stand tall for yourself and your sisters. Let's start with the Moby Dick of diminishers: the antimentor.

Who are these people, and why do we listen to them?

There's a point during my talk on leadership when I say this: "I'm going to say a term . . . antimentor." This is when the mood radically shifts. I follow up with, "I'm guessing someone, or several people, just came to mind. Unfortunately, this word hits a very specific chord for most of us, even if we don't know exactly what it means."

After I say this, people laugh nervously, hold back tears, or smile and nod wisely. No one is neutral.

antimentor /ˈan(t)ē,ˈanˌtī/ /ˈmenˌtôr,ˈmenˌtər/
Someone who should be one of your greatest cheerleaders but who usually leaves you feeling off balance and small.

There isn't a human alive who hasn't fought to overcome, or is still fighting, the buttons (or triggers) installed by their antimentors. Those buttons are the harmful messages that continue to grow like ruthless, pernicious weeds in your mind, even if you are wildly successful in almost every aspect of your life. If you don't learn to quiet them, they run the risk of consuming you, thwarting hopes and dreams.

So, how do we neutralize our antimentors? The first step is identifying them. You would think this would be easy. Nope. While someone popped into your head at the word "antimentor," identifying them can be painfully hard. This is because some antimentors are less charged and easy to spot. For other folks, however, we spend our lives trying to convince ourselves that they are not our antimentors. We suffer a lot from this damaging self-delusion.

Wow! That's Why I Feel like the Incredible Shrinking Woman around This Person!

To identify your antimentors, check out this handy list.

ANTIMENTORS

* Are important people in our lives we usually share a long history with.

* Often have more power than us, or at least the relationship started out that way—think a coach, professor, parent, or involved aunt!

* Usually knew us long before we had a clue we could be superheroes.

* Are profoundly uncomfortable with us when we are in full superhero mode.

* Would never admit to themselves that their identity is wrapped up in us never finding out we are wearing a cape, much less that they are standing on it—they are unconsciously invested in our failure but would never admit this to themselves.

* Often boast of our accomplishments in public, sometimes claiming them as a product of their support, yet oddly in private they bad-mouth those very accomplishments.

* Act like we are behaving out of character when we feel confident and happy.

* Plant criticism like weeds with small, hard-to-pin-down comments that grow whether we water them or not.

* Often are in our inner circle, but we just can't seem to kick them out.

* Can be warm and genuinely supportive with other people, which can make us feel more than a little crazy: "What's wrong with *us*?"

* Are the last people we should listen to, *ever*, and yet we can't help craving their approval the most.

* Are the emotional snipers in our lives, their bullets flying at us with laser-like focus, seemingly out of the blue, hitting their mark every damn time with the stealth precision of a seasoned assassin. In other words . . . ouch.

Much of this chapter will be spent on the most damaging subcategory of antimentors, a group I call inner-circle snipers, or ICSs. These are folks we've known really well, for a long time, and are often part of our inner circle of friends or extended family. Sometimes we're entangled financially with them. (That's truly all kinds of terrible.) It's tempting to ignore how dysfunctional our relationships are with the ICSs in our lives. Acknowledging the problem means you have to finally deal with it. Dealing with it is going to hurt, but we ignore them at our peril.

We should steer clear of our ICSs. Instead, we give them a bullhorn in our headspace.

Why do we do this? *Why?*

We do this because our inner critics are often nurtured, and sometimes birthed, by our antimentors. In many ways, many of us have allowed these folks to define us. So, if they finally approve of us, that can feel more validating than if our cheerleaders tell us we did a great job. We adopt the thinking, "Oh, our cheerleaders are supportive so we can't trust them, but if our critics think we did a good job, then *that* must be real."

The great irony of this is that most of the time it is our cheerleaders who see us much more clearly than our antimentors, because they see the best of us. They inspire us to be our best selves. When we are at our worst, that is not who we are at our core. When we tap our full potential, we are our most true selves. This is why we want to surround ourselves with folks who see us at our best. They see us clearly, unlike our antimentors, who see a negative, distorted view of us.

A Case Study

Last year I was asked to give a keynote address at a Girl Up conference. Girl Up is an organization started by the United Nations to empower girls. The talk went really well, and the news coverage was fantastic.

So, what did I do soon after the talk? Call the most supportive people in my life? Relish the moment? Noooo. That would make sense, but nope. I had a list of people to call, including Dad and Stepmom, but the first person I called was my antimentor, Rich. Rich looms large in my extended family and spent a lot of time crushing my soul growing up. So of course, I had to call him.

Why? *Why?!* Well, here's what was going through my head: "Maybe *this time* Rich will be supportive! How could he possibly find fault with this?"

So, like Charlie Brown running headlong toward the football, I called.

Here's how things went down:

Rich: "Hi Eliza! So, how'd Girl Up go?"

Me: "It went really well!"

Rich: "Wonderful."

Me: "Thanks. It was so fun!"

Rich: "I'm sure. Well, if you want to hear a really powerful woman speak, listen to Elizabeth Warren's speech from this weekend. She was amazing. Now she's a powerful woman."*

They say that insanity is doing the same thing over and over and expecting a different result. By this standard, calling Rich was straight-up insane.

So, why did I do it?

Rich knows how to push every damn one of my buttons because, well, he was one of the adults who installed them. A lot of therapy has taught me exactly what behavior to expect from Rich, yet in my most insecure moments I can still find myself seeking his approval.

Why? Why do we yearn for our ICS approval like drug addicts who just can't quit their habit?

The answer can be summarized in two words: intermittent reinforcement. Intermittent reinforcement is inconsistently rewarding someone regardless of their behavior. Here's a common example: You are doing all kinds of great things. Person A praises you randomly and not often. Person B praises you consistently for your accomplishments. You will go back to person A over and over again. Rare inconsistent rewards psychologically condition us to come back for more. This is what casinos use to hook gamblers. This is why the house always wins. And this is why gamblers leave broken, penniless, wondering why the hell they couldn't just walk out the door—they are addicted.

We are addicted to our antimentors, even those of us who are no longer in denial that these folks are bad for us. Antimentors keep us small and diminished, and it's next to impossible to communicate like a superhero when we feel this way.

Kicking the habit is one of the most critical steps to claiming space like a superhero. But how do we get our antimentors to step off our cape?

Bulletproofing Yourself from Antimentors

Identify the antimentors in your life. This will not be a delightful process. We care about these folks or they would have been gone long ago. If the antimentor checklist didn't do the trick, there is another way to figure out who they are. Check in with your feelings. If you constantly look for someone's approval, rarely get it, and often feel demoralized by them, that's a neon sign flashing ANTIMENTOR! Don't ignore it.

Let go and *do not* look to them for approval. (Again, easier said than done, but definitely possible.) Do this by following these steps:

1. **Remind.** Remind yourself that you will receive constructive feedback from your antimentor only intermittently, but the vast majority of the feedback will be diminishing and negative.

2. **Mourn.** Allow yourself to get really, really sad that your antimentor just can't support you in the way you so wish they would. This can feel like a bit of a death. I wanted to put a joke here to lighten that last sentence, but it's not funny. It hurts.

3. **Release.** Letting go of the hope your antimentor will magically start supporting you can be one of the hardest things you go through in life. You may need a therapist to help you work through it, especially if said antimentor is your parent or someone you expect will support you.

4. **Create.** Once you have really let go of your desire for your antimentor to be a real mentor, start looking for kinder, wiser

people to fill that void. Create a new group of positive mentors who can support you and give constructive feedback, rather than shredding your soul. Some people reading this may think they're too old to find a mentor. You are never too old to find new mentors, and not all of them have to be older than you. As a coach and teacher, I have mentored plenty of people older than me, and I have been mentored by people younger than me. Get creative, think of what kind of person might fill the void, and start forging relationships. Remember, as I said in the beginning of this book, you have only wasted time if you don't learn from your mistakes and do things differently. Finding a new mentor is an excellent way to put this idea into practice.

5. **Push the abort button.** You're not out of the woods yet. When you're at your weakest, the pull to seek out your antimentor for support, support you will never get, magnifies. If this happens, resist! Do not engage, and push the abort button! The abort button is complex, so I've broken it into steps.

   a. **Identify.** Can you identify a slight, undeniable, familiar feeling of unease, dread, worry, or insecurity?

   b. **Listen.** Do not ignore your feelings! Listen—that's the sound of your abort button buzzing. Push it and abort!

   c. **Remind.** Remind yourself that despite the authority you've given your antimentor, their opinions hold no more merit than anyone else's. Indeed, they don't really see you, so their opinions hold a hell of a lot less weight. You don't need their feedback. You can and must abort.

   d. **Reward.** You've been conditioned to go to your antimentor even when you shouldn't. It's time to condition yourself to do the opposite behavior—to associate *not* seeking out your antimentor with a reward. If you love ice cream, eat some. If yoga is your thing, go put your body in the shape of a pretzel. If you got a great review from work, reread it whilst sipping your favorite tea. Reward yourself in some large or small way. Really, take the time to do this. You will train yourself to associate *not calling* your antimentor with a feeling of happiness. Not calling mentor = yummy ice cream. Not calling your mentor = going to a movie. And so on.

Ignore or Call Out the Snipe

Sometimes you can't, or don't want to, avoid engaging with an antimentor. They may be a family member or a coach, and you don't want to quit your family or your team. If this is the case, my IC approach can protect you when they invariably go for the jugular. I love this acronym. When you say it out loud, it sounds like "I see," which reminds me that *I see* what my antimentor is doing, and therefore they shall not mess with me anymore. Here is what IC stands for:

1. **I (ignore).** Don't engage. Don't get reactive. When the sniper fires, be like Neo in *The Matrix*. Stop the bullet in midair by saying to yourself, "Ah, antimentor, sniping yet again, and oh so predictable. This is simply what they do." Then change the subject. When people don't get reactions, they often eventually give up poking. Stop those bullets before they land, like Neo would. Remember, "There is no spoon." Or for those who, for some tragic reason, have not watched *The Matrix*, "If I understand my antimentor's emotional coding, then I can hear their snipes but the bullets can't land."

2. **C (call it out).** Antimentors, fundamentally, are bullies, and bullies are cowards. Calling them out will stop their behavior in the present and prevent it in the future. So, if you can't stop the bullet by ignoring it, call it out, or it will remain firmly lodged in you.

   There are two ways to do this:

   a. **Question.** First, try asking a question; for example, "I'm confused. Are you comparing me unfavorably to Elizabeth

Warren as I'm sharing my excitement about my talk with you?" This will cause your antimentor to have to explain themselves. Usually, they will backtrack, apologize, and say that is not what they meant, even though it actually was. If they say, "Oh no, that's not what I meant at all!" just say, "Oh, good. I'm glad to hear it." Hopefully this gentle callout will put them on warning and reduce future snipes.

b. **Name.** If you want to take a more direct approach in the hopes of more permanently shutting them down, try naming the snipe without apology. Scary? Yes. Do it anyway. Be brave! If you don't call people on bad behavior, it will probably keep happening. For example, "You saying Elizabeth Warren is a 'real' powerful woman makes me feel like you're saying I'm not." Sometimes they will backtrack. Occasionally, however, they will own it. "Yes, you nailed it. That's exactly what I meant." If this happens, you have now created space for sharing your feelings in a long overdue conversation. This will be hard, and it will be transformative.

See, Then Forgive

When you really *see* people, they can lose their power over you. How many strong, happy, centered folks do you know who go around eviscerating people? I would guess zero. So it stands to reason your antimentors are fragile and are suffering. People in this state are simply unable to do the right thing. I have had conversations with folks who told me, in so many words, they were antimentors in someone's life. Some blamed their mentee; others blamed themselves. All seemed trapped in a permanent state of terrible, gut-wrenching pain. When you see your antimentor as a flawed human, they will lose most of their power. This, in turn, will empower you. Perhaps just as importantly, when you're ready, seeing their pain will allow you to do something incredibly healing for you both: begin to forgive them.

One More Word about Antimentors

I love the following quote. My heart sometimes fights the power of Dr. Angelou's words, but my head knows they are true. When it comes to antimentors, our heads must work diligently to protect our vulnerable hearts.

> My dear, why must you be shown twenty-nine times before you can see who they really are? Why can't you get it the first time? When people show you who they are, believe them.
>
> —DR. MAYA ANGELOU, talking to her mentee . . . Oprah Winfrey

"I'm proud of you." These simple words are all that we want from our antimentors. We will never hear them when we need them. Let go of hoping your antimentors will say these words. If you do, something miraculous will happen. You will make room for another voice, one that not only believes those words, but will be there for you, like a rock. This person's unwavering support will embolden and empower you to realize your full potential. That person, you may have guessed, is you. The greatest gift our antimentors can give us is learning that, in the end, our own voice is the only voice that really matters.

So take your antimentor's boot off your cape and find the power within you to fly.

Or as Glinda said to Dorothy in *The Wizard of Oz*, like the good mentor she was, "*You* always had the power, my dear; you just had to learn it for yourself."

When Words Don't Matter

Beyond mentors, there is another category of folks who can do a lot of damage, slowly turning your harmonious, connected friends or coworkers into an unpleasant quagmire of fear, anger, and discord. I'm talking about the type of people who seem so appealing at first, but soon enough it becomes clear they could turn the best of friends against each other, or exhaust Oprah's empathy, or make Black Widow give up a fight. They make it hard for you to claim space for yourself and, by extension, claim space with others.

These scary people share one trait: *their words don't matter*. They talk a great game, but their behavior tells a very different story. Know that you are playing with fire if you network with, become friends with, date, partner with, or collaborate with these folks. Here are the words-don't-matter archetypes so you can easily spot those folks and never fall for their smooth-as-silk silver tongues again.

TYPE 1: THE EMOTIONAL VAMPIRE

Definition: Unhappy people who suck your time and emotional energy.

Words: I just need to talk to you about this *one* thing.

Action: It's never just one thing.

Telltale phrases:

"Only you can help me!" (Others can.)

"It'll only take a few minutes!" (Not true.)

Friends laugh with us, cry with us, and sometimes seek our support. In turn, they support us when we need them. Emotional vampires are not that friend. They relentlessly, unceasingly suck every last reserve of our emotional energy and time. Fall in with a vampire and you will become that husk of a woman. You won't exercise for weeks. You will snap at your kids. You will find yourself skipping critical meetings while sitting in Starbucks as your vampire cries inconsolably (and I mean *inconsolably*) over her nonfat Frappuccino with extra whipped cream, chocolate sauce, and a little drizzle of caramel.

How to spot an emotional vampire:

- They are prone to hyperbole: "Oh. My. God. This is the worst day of my *life*!!!" (It's not.)

- They phone bomb you, beginning every phone call with "I just need to ask one thing!" (And by "one thing," they mean many.)

97

- They make grand promises about changing and growing: "*Amazing* advice! I'm *totally* going to use it to change this time!" (They do believe they will, but unless they get serious therapy, they most definitely will not.)

- They rarely ask about your life, except to say, "I hope you're doing well," before launching into their current crises. (They genuinely want to care, but their own seemingly gigantic struggles dwarf all interest in others.)

- They are masterful guilt trippers about your availability: "Don't feel bad if you can't talk to me. I'm OK. Really. I don't need to talk. [Sniff. Sniff.]" (They do want you to feel bad so you'll talk to them for the one hundredth time.)

In the words of my friend Hadiyah, who went from a coffee-slinging barista to CEO of a well-known café chain on the West Coast, "You know Eliza, when people figure out you're good at something, they'll ask you to keep doing it until you tell them to stop." Part of why Hadiyah is so successful is she regularly tells emotional vampires to stop. She doesn't have angst about it, and she isn't mean. She simply says, firmly but kindly, "I can't do that right now."

Emotional vampires very quickly figure out who they can suck the life out of and who they can't. The light at the end of the vampire tunnel is that most are conflict averse, abhorring direct communication. You need only set a boundary, and they will move on. If you want to gain hours of free time, tell emotional vampires in your life to stop. Your future self, the less stressed version of you who actually gets to the gym and doesn't dread her phone ringing, will thank you.

TYPE 2: THE INSPIRING LEADER WHO ABANDONS SHIP

Definition: Inspiring, brilliant leaders who make big promises, have great ideas, embark on lofty projects, but don't finish what they start.

Words: I have a great idea! Follow me!

Actions: None—they can't follow through.

Telltale phrases:

"I'm really going to finish this project."

"This time will be different!"

"I'm finally ready! I'm *ready*! Whoo!"

"Wanna join my team?"

Meet Serena. Serena is a moderately attractive woman in her early thirties. By moderately attractive, I mean she is five feet ten; has a huge head of shiny, luxurious, fire-engine-red curly hair; has cheekbones that could cut glass; and has green eyes I thought only existed if you were wearing those weird fake contact lenses. She is one of the smartest people I've ever met and has the charisma of former president Reagan, Taylor Swift, and a snake-oil salesperson all rolled into one. I've known Serena since we were in middle school. Watching her speak has always been like watching a superhero show off her most impressive, mind-blowing superpower.

Serena has a passion for film, which she studied in school, and is an incredibly talented writer and director. For years she would write scripts, find collaborators, and embark upon ambitious film projects. Serena would often ask me to edit her latest fascinating screenplay, and I would do it happily. The shoot would go well. Serena had several editors at her beck and call, and one would invariably deliver a fantastic fine cut at a steep discount. Then the moment would come—time to stop fiddling, lock the film, and release it.

Here's what would predictably happen next.

Serena would pull the plug on the film, or at least put it into a permanent coma. She'd look over the fine cut and decide that something *just wasn't right*. Then I'd start to hear phrases like this:

"You know, I'm just missing a shot I really need."

"Something just doesn't feel ready about it."

"I don't know if this is the caliber I want out there."

She would never release it. Her films would sit on her hard drive, gathering dust, while her frustrated collaborators thought to themselves, "Argh! This time I really thought things would be different!"

How to spot inspiring leaders who abandon ship:

- They are charming.

- They have an almost magical way with words.

- They are aces at making up excuses about their lack of follow through.

- They have contagious excitement about projects, which always get dropped.

- They are usually creative, energetic, well-meaning people who intend to follow through, which is how they are able to convince others that they will.

We have all known leaders who were great starters, motivators, and collaborators but terrible finishers. This archetype tends to be tragically terrified of failure. This results in a quest for perfection, which ultimately sabotages their success. Their fear ironically causes them to fail. You, their collaborators, become collateral damage.

Before you ever consider working with someone on a project that could potentially sap your time or your money, be absolutely sure to look at what has actually happened with this person's past collaborations. Look for results, rather than listening to enticing words. Never jump on anyone's dead-end journey. Not ever.

TYPE 3: THE FAIR-WEATHER FRIEND

Definition: That person who professes that they are your rock, but during hard times they bail.

Words: I'm here for you. I'm your best friend.

Actions: When the going gets tough, they head for the hills.

Telltale phrases:

"Whatever you need, no matter what, just call."

"I'll be there for you!"

"I will drop anything, and I mean anything, for you."

The confusing thing about this archetype is that before a crisis hits, you can't always predict if they will or won't be there for you. They talk such a fantastic game! We can be fooled until that unfortunate moment comes when we really need them and they aren't there.

How to spot the fair-weather friend:

- They aren't there when you really need them.

- Again

- And again.

- And again and again.

Fair-weather friends can actually be a wonderful part of our lives, as long as you don't count on them when the going gets tough. If you can become OK with this, you might be able to appreciate the qualities they bring to your life during the fun, easy, good times. If you want to pursue a casual friendship, I recommend inviting them to a softball game or casual drinks with a big group of friends. They'll be fantastic company until you slice open your finger on a broken wine glass and need a ride to the hospital.

TYPE 4: THE PEOPLE PLEASER

Definition: People who say yes to everything then get really resentful because they wanted to say no.

Words: I'm happy to do that for you.

Actions: I probably won't do it and almost certainly will talk serious smack about you for asking.

Telltale phrases:

"Happy to do that!" Even when they're not.

"I totally agree with you!" Even when they don't.

"That doesn't bother me at *all*." Even when it does.

People pleasers desperately need to be liked. By everyone. Even people who are acting like assholes. You can be a complete jerk to a people pleaser and they will show little to no sign that your behavior is unacceptable. You will get the impression they're the nicest people you've ever met as they are always so damn nice, so easygoing. Eventually you will learn they are biting their tongues constantly and thus full of simmering rage. Then all hell breaks loose . . . but behind your back.

How to spot a people pleaser:

- They self-identify as "nice."
- They are "other" focused to a fault.
- They are oleaginous backstabbers.
- They fear direct communication.
- They are consistently conflict averse.
- They interpret forthright as hostile.
- They seem like everyone's best friend.
- They are overcommitted and underperforming.
- They are prone to truth-stretching or outright lying.
- They rarely say no without excuses or blaming others.

This archetype is seemingly warm and friendly, but in the immortal words of my brilliant friend Kim, "People pleasers will kill you and cry over your dead body." Steer clear.

TYPE 5: JEKYLL AND HYDE ABUSER

Definition: People who hurt you but say they care about you. These folks are in the closest inner circle of our network . . . our intimate relationships.

Words: I love you. Forever and ever.

Actions: Physical/emotional abuse and in some cases abrupt abandonment. (The emotional abuse can be very hard to spot.)

Telltale phrases (and phases):

Idealize phase

"I'm a nice guy."

"You're absolutely perfect."

"You are my soul mate!"

"I've only known you for less than a week, but *I love you forever!*"

"We're exactly the *same!*"

"You are the most amazing person I've ever met in my *entire life.*"

"OK, we're different, but I guess that's OK!"

"You're sane—not crazy like all of my exes. They have all blocked me. Bitches!"

Devalue/diminish phase

"You know, we're way too different."

"You are demanding too much!"

"Actually, you're completely different from me! You tricked me!"

"Why are you so sensitive/illogical/hormonal?"

Abuse or discard phase

"You've changed! You are such a crazy/imperfect bitch!!!"

"If I emotionally abuse/hurt/hit you, it's your fault."

"I will never ignore/devalue/diminish/hurt you again. Hello, eternal love!"

"You aren't the woman I thought you were. Bye."

Consider yourself lucky if you hear that last phrase. This is, hands down, the most dangerous archetype. They are damaged, and their response to that damage is to hurt others. Learn to spot them and avoid them.

How to spot a Jekyll and Hyde abuser:

- The phrases I've already listed are a pretty good indicator. In that order.

- They move in fast with a torrent of "love" (search online for "love bombing").

- They are controlling of your actions and sometimes your beliefs.

- They run unpredictably hot and cold.

- They praise you for putting up with their bad behavior.

- You start to question your values and even your reality at times.

- The abuse doesn't happen overnight but instead slowly escalates.

- You can't figure out why you are still with them.

- They break your heart. Again and again.

- They hurt you emotionally and/or physically.

- They will leave you the very moment you need them the most.

The issue of physical and emotional abuse is beyond the scope of this book. I included it because, at best, being in a romantic relationship with a disordered person makes it close to impossible to fully claim space. At worst, it can kill you.

If you have lived through the idealize-devalue-discard stages of abuse, I suggest reading any book on narcissism or sociopathy. There are also useful online resources. (Surviving Narcissism is a current standout.)

If you feel like you are in emotional or physical danger, go to the National Domestic Abuse Hotline online. You can contact and get help from them with complete anonymity. If you want to learn more about the tragic national crisis of domestic violence, I strongly recommend you read the powerful book *No Visible Bruises* by Rachel Louise Snyder. It should be required reading for every woman, and every man, in this country. (Overall, women are abused more in relationships, but we do not have a monopoly on this problem. People of all genders are susceptible to abusive relationships.[1])

Overall, seek out help from a therapist if the telltale phrases look familiar, and remember, if someone tries to separate you from your sisters . . . *run*.

So, that's the list. Once you start seeing these folks, you can't unsee them.

One last thing . . . if you see yourself in these archetypes, don't panic. I believe very few people try to be cruel or happily identify as evil. If we work from this premise, these archetypes *are not* able to see themselves very well. If you *are* able to see some of yourself in these types, you probably haven't fallen prey to the dark side. Continue working on yourself, and be happy you have the self-awareness needed not to crush the souls of others.

That said, if one category describes you uncomfortably well, take heart. For years, I was almost a full-blown people pleaser. Eventually, I was able to self-reflect. Today, that less-than-optimal part of myself is pretty much vanquished. All hope is never lost!

When to Leave Any Relationship

This is a short section because in most cases we make this a lot more complicated than it should be. If there is someone in your life who seems to decrease your sense of self-worth and who doesn't fall into one of the categories I outlined, here is a handy way to identify those folks.

First, let's start with the easy part. What factors should you never use to make this determination? Before making a decision, resist trying to prove to yourself that the person is

* Always wrong
* Too different from you

* Making you feel nuts on purpose
* Trying to hurt you
* Gaslighting you by accident
* Impossible to get along with
* A little crazy
* A lot crazy
* Mean
* Evil to the core

So, how do you decide if you should walk or not? You don't need to judge the person. You don't need to prove that in every disagreement they were very wrong and you were very right.

You just need to determine three things:

1. How much am I willing or able to compromise/change?
2. How much are they willing or able to compromise/change?
3. Is the point where we land something I can, and want to, tolerate?

One hint that you don't want to tolerate something is when you are constantly wondering about point 3. If you are giving an inordinate amount of thought to "Should I stay or should I go?" you probably already know the answer. If that's where you're at, then give this some thought: Short-term pain hurts. Long-term pain is just short-term pain extended over years of suffering. It wears you down and destroys your life.

Short-term pain doesn't last forever, and you almost always have to go through it to live pain free in the long run. So boldly make your decision, act on it, and stick with it. Full stop. Soon enough, "Damn, this hurt like hell" will turn into "Why the hell didn't I do this sooner?"

FORGE CONNECTION

Create your justice league! You're feeling good, you've neutralized individuals who would make you small, now for the fun part: forging connection! The best way to raise up other women is to connect with them. When we are connected to people, we help them, and they help us! Here's how you go about it.

Networking Is the Foundation That Builds Up Women

Let's start out with networking. What exactly is networking? Why does it matter? And what is the best way to network?

Networking is simply forming connections through family, friends, work, and play that have the potential to help you. Find women who you can support and who support you. You will always have a sister to celebrate with; you will never face hardship alone; you will do better in both your career and your personal life.

NETWORKING: THE BASICS FOR POWERHOUSE SPACE CLAIMERS

Here are some fundamentals of networking:

* **Be authentic.** Connections should be ethical and come from an actual desire to know someone. If you don't like someone, don't network with them.

* **Seek people out.** Always be on the lookout for people you genuinely like, and work to forge relationships with them. You might find them in unexpected places. I met one of my favorite people, Darryle Johnson, on my kids' playground. At the time he was working as a teacher's aide. He ended up being one of my most talented acting students. Today I'm fortunate to count him as one of my closest friends, and we have collaborated on several projects together. He always makes me look amazing! Had I not been open to striking up a conversation with a man younger than me who I didn't know from Adam while picking up my kid from school, I would have missed out on a lifelong friendship with a truly spectacular human.

* **Be attentive.** Tend to your relationships in proportion to how deep you want them to go. You don't have to spend a lot of time with everyone. Networking can feel like a huge task, and it does take time. But it should be fun. If you don't want to spend a lot of time with someone, but you like them and value them as a part of your network, keep in touch via social media and invite them to your house when you have a larger function.

* **Connect others.** Introduce, introduce, introduce. The more you connect people in your network, the more valuable you become to your network. I am always looking for ways to connect women with other women. (And men as well!) One way to do this en masse is to think of your friends who would like each other, and invite them to your place. I do this often, and you don't have to kill yourself getting ready. Keep it casual with a dish to pass and inexpensive with bring-your-own

booze (or kombucha, or seltzer, or whatever it is you drink if you don't "drink"). The night starts with all of us sharing our business cards and saying what we do, then we just have fun. It's a great way to deepen connections and help others while spending time with interesting people.

* **Offer value.** Give before taking and give more than you get. Think of how you can give back to your network regularly. The more you give, the more you get. And giving feels good!

* **Seek diversity.** Make sure your network has people not just from different races, genders, ages, and so on, but from different careers. The more diversified your network is, the more you can connect people with others who can help them, which brings me to . . .

* **Network with men.** Believe it or not, one way to support other women is by networking with men. Men statistically have more power and money. If you can find a man interested in raising you up because of your worth, not your face, wonderful! As you rise you will be in a better position to raise other women. Also, men have different experiences than we do, which is important. Alek Osinski is my little-brother-from-another-mother, one of my three closest friends, and an amazing human. We learn so much from each other's perspectives.

* **Join and create.** Men have been golfing together for years! Figure out what you like to do and do it! Join a volleyball league, political campaign, or radical anarchist knitting club. When you join groups, you will find people with similar interests. Most likely those are the folks you want in your network. If you like underwater basket weaving, and there is no such club, create one. This can be harder to do if you are married in a heterosexual relationship because statistically women still do more housework, so we have less time to weave baskets underwater. This is a good moment to claim the space you need in your relationship! You have the right to do *only* 50 percent of the housework, and you have the right to spend

time out of the home just as much as your husband. Settle for no less. Weave that basket.

✳ **Be kind.** More on this at the end of the chapter, but this is the best way to network. Meet people and be a decent human—it goes a long way, and you will attract the right people to your network.

And finally, my personal favorite . . .

✳ **Drink more beer; skip more work!** This critical point was inspired by Adira, a brilliant young engineer who came to me soon after starting her new job. She wanted guidance on how to get ahead. She had joined the firm with one other woman and four men at about the same time. She didn't understand what she was doing wrong. One or two times a week she was asked to go to lunch with some of the men she worked with, two of whom were in upper management. And every Friday at about 3:00 p.m., she was asked to play a board game in the afternoon with the same folks. She was proud that she said no. She felt that would prove to them she was a hard worker and the extra time would allow her to be more productive. I told her to forget about being productive and that it was much more important she spend time socializing.

Indeed, my exact words were, "Adira, drink more beer. Skip more work." Adira was skeptical. To her the idea of going out to lunch and having cocktails, thus making it hard for her to work the rest of the day, was unthinkable. It seemed completely counterintuitive. As a woman, didn't she need to prove herself? Eventually, I convinced her to give it a chance. She tried it. Within three months she was promoted. To be clear, I don't think this is a great thing. In an ideal world you would be promoted because of your productivity and work ethic, and yet, it is a *true* thing. Your network is, as they say, your net worth.

Also, keep in mind that while lunch and board games are innocuous, every offer from male management to a new female employee to hang out does not immediately need to be accepted. This is especially true if there is any question at all about the man's intentions.

First Impressions: Greet like a Boss

Networking is, at its core, connecting with people, and once people form an initial impression of you, it's very hard to walk back from that impression. You will attract powerful people into your life when you lead with power. Here's how to do that right from the start.

Making a great first impression is critical. It sends a clear message to people about who you are and how you expect to be treated. There is no room for being small when you first meet someone. You need to throw down your expectations about how the relationship will move forward like a boss. You must expand your presence, not contract it.

Throw It Down Right from the Start!

The following are the three component parts to those first few seconds when you meet someone. Master all three and you set the stage for an equitable, respectful relationship where you can expand without fear of pushback.

YOUR EYES

Eye contact is critical, and for introverts, sustained eye contact with a new person can be very, very challenging. If you are an introvert, follow this advice I give to my clients: if your eyes don't feel like they are on fire, you are probably doing it wrong.

* **Don't look down.** When I role play first meetings with my clients, particularly women, they often look down at the floor several times while moving in for the initial handshake. This immediately sets up an uneven power dynamic, and you will not be the one on top.

* **Don't blink.** Many people respond to not looking down by suddenly blinking rapidly. Rapid blinking makes you look untrustworthy.

* **Maintain eye contact.** Look at the other person, holding their gaze. You will look confident even if you're not.

For some, all of this may feel a bit odd. People don't have this level of intense eye contact in everyday life very often. If you feel a little odd, you are most definitely doing it right.

YOUR BODY

Claim space by opening up your body. Some women have a tendency to physically shrink when meeting new people. It's a way of saying, "Don't hurt me! I'm not threatening." Of course, if some people think they can boss you around, they most certainly will. Never, ever shrink when first meeting someone.

* **Make sure you have excellent posture.** By now you have read the chapter on standing tall, so this shouldn't be a problem!

* **Keep your face open and at least moderately friendly.** I'm not advocating a nervous, diminishing perma-smile here. Nerves can cause us to scowl or squint. Unless you're trying to scare the person, try to avoid this.

* **Smile.** Yup, I just told women to smile. OK, I realize women are told to smile all the time, even when they have every reason not to. I realize men are not expected to smile. I realize this double standard is unfair. That said, I don't believe women should be less friendly and smile less when greeting people . . . I believe men should be friendlier and smile more! My clients of all genders make better impressions, resulting in better outcomes, when they smile during those first critical seconds. That said, if smiling goes against your belief system, I do get it. If you can make not smiling work for you, please email me

with all the details. I love to be proven wrong. Disclaimer: I will shamelessly steal your strategies.

✳ **A strong handshake.** I owe my firm handshake to my dad, who drilled handshaking badassery into my head from the time I was a little girl. When I was growing up, my dad was high up in our local government. His position offered him plenty of opportunities to introduce me to reporters or other leaders in our community. "Go ahead, Eliza!" he'd say proudly. "Say hello and introduce yourself with a nice firm handshake!" Today, I relish that moment when I shake a man's hand as firmly as he shakes mine. At first they usually look a bit surprised, but immediately their surprise morphs into respect. Women tend to have weaker, more tentative handshakes than men. This is a real handicap—it's as if we are starting every interaction by showing our necks. Here's how to shake hands like my dad taught me. (Thanks, Thys VanCort, a.k.a. Dad!)

- Match the strength of your handshake with the person you're meeting. (This will be readily apparent!)

- If their handshake is very weak, be just a little stronger. (Unless your goal is to intimidate, which can be a legit goal at times, don't crush their hand.)

- If someone seems bent on breaking your hand, game *on!* (When this happens to me, I squeeze their hand as hard as I possibly can until they back down. This may feel aggressive. It is, but so is attempting to crush someone's bones.)

Even though a strong handshake is a relatively aggressive communication posture, handshakes are the one piece of communication where overt aggression rarely has negative consequences for women. I have never experienced pushback from someone after laying on my strongest vice grip, nor have my clients. We've only been treated with more respect.

YOUR COMMUNICATION

The final component to claiming space with others is twofold. Firstly, own yourself by owning your name. Names have great power. Embrace that power. Secondly, understand the nature of help and don't think of it as a bad word. Help builds community. Community sustains us.

Say Your Name with Conviction!

There is no more important moment than when you tell someone your name. How you say it will have as much or more impact than the quality of your handshake. Here are the two things to remember about the verbal component of introductions.

✳ **Say it loud.** Say your chosen introductory platitude, "How nice to meet you!" for example, with a volume slightly louder than you speak in conversational speech. Most importantly, *do not* speak more quietly than usual, as some of us are apt to do, especially in high-stakes introductions.

✳ **Say it proud.** I said it in my TEDx. I say it when giving talks or running workshops. I say it when coaching and when parenting my kids. *Your name is your power!* Mumbling when saying your name, or allowing someone to mispronounce your name, is the first step on the slippery slope of ceding your power to another human. Often people mispronounce my name. They say "Uh-liza" or "Ah-liza" rather than "Eeeeliza." When I was younger, I'd let it slide. Today, I always take a moment to be sure folks say my name as Mary Louise Marini VanCort, my mama, intended. "Actually, it's Eeeeliza." When I first started doing this, I worried that asking folks to say my name correctly would result in some sort of *Mad Max*–worthy communication apocalypse. Much to my delight, quite the opposite happened. As with a firm handshake, I was treated with more respect.

You tell a story about who you are, how you feel about yourself, and exactly how much space you believe you have a right to claim every time you look into someone's eyes for the first time, reaching out your hand to shake theirs. Be sure the story you're telling is the one you want to tell. Let your message always be this: "It's nice to meet you. My name is _____. I'm comfortable in my skin, and I'm your equal. Treat me as such, and I'll do the same for you."

Greet like a boss. You'll be treated like a boss.

Asking for Help Doesn't Mean You're Incompetent

One of the best ways to know your value is to ask for help. I realize this might sound counterintuitive, but it is not. There are two ways to ask.

1. **Vertical help**: asking people who have more or less power than you.
2. **Horizontal help**: asking people who have the same power as you.

Vertical Help, More Power

Asking for help from someone who has more power than you can be daunting, but *do it*! It's a really fantastic way to build relationships with other women. It also can help you forge all kinds of relationships, including powerful mentor relationships. If you need help from someone who is more powerful than you, you're probably going to them for a connection or advice. Most people like to talk about what they're good at and what they have knowledge about. One of the best ways to forge connection with a person is to say, "Hey Person, you know a lot about a lot of stuff! Can you tell me about that stuff?" If you want your boss or your connected neighbor or your distant aunt to be part of your circle, ask them to share their knowledge with you. Most people enjoy showing off what they know. Of course, there are notable exceptions, but those are probably not the people you want to be going to in the first place. Think antimentors.

Finally, asking people in another field, or folks you don't know well, to teach/mentor you is fine, but it is a big ask and can be a lot of labor. Be sure they are excited to share and don't see it as a burden. The purpose is to forge connection, not stress people out.

Horizontal Help

Horizontal help happens with colleagues at work and friendships in life. People tend to hesitate to do this because they feel they are being a burden. I will talk a lot about flipping the script in the upcoming chapters, but for now just think to yourself, "Self, would I be fine with someone coming to me and asking for this help? Would I feel thankful they trusted me enough to ask?" If the answer is yes and yes, ask. Why is it OK for others to ask, but somehow it's not OK for you? Know your worth, claim some space, and ask!

Vertical Help, Less Power

Vertical help comes largely in the form of delegating. Women often take on work outside of their job description. Vertical help is critical because if you don't do it, you will end up doing everyone's work for them. No human can do this, so balls will be dropped. Good leaders delegate. Not only does that make your life easier, but it shows people you trust them with important tasks. Build connection by empowering others with your trust.

On the flip side, when my dear friend Kira Sholeen Wagner read this, she said, "I have realized that because I am an excellent problem solver, they rely on me too much and take credit for my work. When I read this, that is where my brain went. Obviously, I'm hypersensitive about vertical help."[1]

Good point, Kira! Be sure you *delegate to others* but be careful. Women are often asked to take on an unfair share of the load. It's vertical help, not vertical exploitation!

Reject Scarcity, Embrace Abundance

This is perhaps the most important thing to remember from this chapter: Claim space ferociously and you will rise up. Rise up, and you have the power to reach down and help other women ascend with you.

Reject the scarcity myth and help other women. Hire women. Defend women. Promote women. Have tea with women. Go dancing with women. Tell your stories. Listen to others' stories. Raise up your daughters' voices. Listen to your mother's stories. Love your sisters. Embrace what makes us the same, and learn from our differences.

And always, always remember that networking is deeper than a work community. It is more inclusive than a group of friends. It is wider than our beloved families. Networking is a mindful act of connectedness. It is a choice to raise other women up. Make that choice. For yourself, and for all of us. We really will rise higher.

PART 3

NEVER CEDE YOUR SPACE

Neutralize kryptonite!

Stop damaging patterns of self-sabotage.

I'm tough, ambitious, and I know exactly what I want. If that makes me a bitch, okay

—MADONNA

The things we say and do, the stories we are told, and the stories we tell serve as the guideposts in our lives. Some are empowering, pushing us to do better, work harder, and never settle. Others do just the opposite. They make us shrink ourselves in order to accommodate other people and situations.

As an unabashed superhero nerd, I think of these negative guideposts as our emotional kryptonite. We can be in a great place in our lives—wonderful friends, thriving careers, great relationships—but this particular form of kryptonite can bring us to our knees.

Women often share similar kryptonite because we share similar training, training that started when we were little girls. We were taught to apologize when someone hurt us. We were taught to "be polite" when our opinions made our parents' guests uncomfortable. We were taught to be quiet and pretty. We were taught that others set the agenda and we need to accommodate. And we are taught that when the Beast comes along, if we can be enough like Beauty, we can turn him into our prince.

I know when I feel powerful. I listen to myself. I trust my instincts. I speak my mind without apology. The thing I struggle with most in my life is not being powerful when things are going well; it's losing myself when confronted with my kryptonite.

These are the moments I get *that* feeling; you know, the feeling something is just not right, tugging at the back of your psyche, telling you to summon your most powerful self and stand your ground. The times when things fall apart for me is when I ignore that voice. It's in those moments that instead of expanding into my power and claiming space, I begin to shrink.

When faced with another human or circumstance that makes us feel weak and small, many of us do not expand into ourselves. We do not proclaim that we will not diminish ourselves for another human being. Instead, we gauge just how small we need to be in order to avoid confrontation. Then we become exactly that small. We stuff our opinions. We shift priorities. We change our behavior. We conflate kind with being nice. We don't embrace "no." We question our worth and claim space with apology. In short, we shrink, ceding our power exactly when we need it most.

Most of us follow a pattern when ceding power (I think of it more as a recipe, as in recipe for disaster).

THE BEST RECIPE FOR CEDING YOUR POWER

1. You do not see the warning signs.

2. You ignore what is happening once you see the warning signs.

3. Eventually you can't ignore what is happening any longer, yet you silence yourself rather than stating your point of view.

4. Once it is over, you beat yourself up for steps 1–3, and because it was so painful, you try not to think about it anymore.

5. Rinse. Repeat.

This part exists for one reason: to give you concrete tools that ensure you will see the warning signs mentioned in step 1, so you never have to live through the endless, painful cycle of steps 2–4.

Part 4 of this book will discuss negative things done to us in spaces. However, before we dive into that challenge, the first thing we must do is examine what we have been trained to do to ourselves that make us small.

We are trained to

✳ Default to nice

✳ Apologize

✳ Devalue our time

✳ Underutilize "no"

✳ Fear words meant to shut us up and make us small

Or, to summarize, we are trained to silence our point of view. There is no better way to keep a woman small than to silence her.

Until a few years ago, I thought most of my kryptonite was fully under control. After a great deal of self-reflection (and therapy!), I had made major changes in my life to claim space. I was single and finally truly happily so. I was enjoying working hard, and my career was thriving in ways I had not thought possible. I often marveled at my life, thanking myself for being brave, for pushing myself out of my comfort zone, for insisting I claim space in the face of great odds. In short, I was embracing life—kicking ass and claiming space like a damn boss.

Then I met Brad.

Ceding Space Not at All like a Boss

I had decided to try out an online dating app. Just a few weeks in, Brad came up on my feed. Brad wasn't tall; I prefer tall men. Brad had a thick head of red hair; I have never been attracted to redheads. To top it off, he was from a suburban family from Cherry Hill, New Jersey—basically another planet compared to my upbringing. However, for the past few years, I had been in a relationship with Daniel, a fascinating and gifted young film-maker twenty years my junior. It ended amicably, and we are still fast friends and collaborators. After such a positive relationship, I thought that perhaps other unexpected love might happen if I gave it the chance.

I reached out to Brad. Very soon after, he got back to me with a long, engaging message. I returned his message, and before I knew it, we were talking on the phone for hours every day.

In the beginning, it was magic. Brad was incredibly accommo-dating, popping over to my house even though he lived an hour and a half away, talking on the phone until the wee hours of the night, even though I found out later he really preferred to go to bed early. He seemed to be exactly who I had been looking for—eerily so. I liked Billy Joel; he liked Billy Joel. I used to sing in an a cappella group; he did as well. After meeting me only three times in person, he told me he had never met anyone like me in his life, I was the woman he'd been waiting for, and yes, it might seem early, but he was madly in love with me.

Then slowly, imperceptibly, I began ceding space, moving the needle on my boundaries. Early on he asked me if he could text me sweet nothings throughout the day. I told him it might actually be distracting for me and maybe we could try to keep texting mostly to after work hours. He happily agreed. A few days later he began texting me during the day. Soon we were texting constantly.

Week by week, little by little, I gave up my power, lowering my standards. The process was so incremental I rationalized that little nagging voice in my head warning me that something was amiss. When I was hospitalized for a week with a condition that seriously threatened my health, Brad came to visit me only once. I never asked Brad to come more often. When he regularly reminded me I wasn't the really thin body type he usually preferred, I did not say, "I'm fit as hell. If you don't like me this way, walk." When he became controlling, asking me to tell him when I would be off the grid writing for a few hours, I should have said one simple word: no. I did not. Eventually his moods began to unpredictably run hot and cold. I adjusted my behavior in the vain hope of avoiding him morphing from an incredibly attentive, thoughtful, kind, loving man to someone I barely recognized—a cold, distant, and diminishing man. I began tolerating behaviors I would once have thought unthinkable, and I kept how much they were hurting me to myself.

Looking back on what was happening toward the end of our relationship, it's still hard for me to believe how much of myself I lost. The last month we were together, Brad asked me to come to his house. He warned me I was not to speak to him for the entire day. He just wanted me around the house while he did chores. When I gently suggested I do them with him, he said I was missing the point. He wanted to do them alone. On top of this, he would be going out with his best friend, Tammy, after his day was done. I could expect to spend thirty to forty-five minutes with him that evening, once he returned home from the bar. When I gently asked what time he was coming home, he said he did not want me putting controlling limits on his time.

In hindsight, the thing that upsets me most is not Brad's request. I have found most of us, even when harming others, do not intend to do harm. We also rarely request things that don't feel reasonable to us. "Hey, I think I'll hurt someone and be totally unreasonable!" isn't the way most humans think. Furthermore, I wasn't in Brad's head. I will never understand his perspective, but I'm guessing if he were telling this story, it would be very, very different. There is, however, one thing I do know that is irrefutable: how his behavior felt to me. Brad's behavior left me feeling incredibly sad, hurt, confused, and angry. From my perspective, it was unreasonable. *I don't have to know Brad's motivation, or his intent.* I don't have to know if he felt his ask was reasonable or unreasonable, kind or cruel. I simply have to know my boundary.

Thankfully, my kryptonite had not yet subsumed my strength. I stayed home that day. Not only was it a really hard decision, but I never clearly shared my anger about how outlandish his request felt. I had allowed myself to become so small. I was not the strong, confident woman I had been only sixteen months earlier when we met. Far from it.

The amazing part is there were red flags from the start. Toward the end, my friends were becoming worried. A dear friend, who is a judge and sees women who have been hurt by toxic relationships, gently recommended a book about unhealthy relationships. And yet, I stayed.

Eventually the time came when I really, really needed Brad for something I would not have thought twice about doing for someone I cared about. He wasn't there. This began a series of events that ended the relationship.

At first, I was devastated. Then I berated myself for being unable to move on emotionally from someone who told me with words and actions he would not have my back. Then I was angry, not at Brad, but at myself.

How had I allowed another human being to make me feel so small? Why had I repeatedly failed to state my needs, despite feeling utterly confused, devalued, and diminished? I was shaken. I understood this stuff! I was a fierce, strong woman who had claimed space like a damn champ before I met this man. What was wrong with me?

I began to forgive myself only after carefully looking backward at my history. That's when I realized the Brads of the world were a perfect dysfunctional fit for me—my childhood, my life experiences, and the messages I had been fed as a woman made Brad the walking embodiment of my emotional kryptonite.

1. I did not see the warning signs.

2. I ignored what was happening once I saw the warning signs.

3. Even once I couldn't ignore them, I silenced myself.

4. Once it was over, I beat myself up for steps 1–3, and it was so painful, I tried not to think about it.

Thankfully, I did not engage in step 5 of the recipe. I did not rinse. I did not repeat.

Instead, I worked (hard!) to do this:

5. Learn. Grow. Change.

Shut up or there will be consequences. Don't state your needs. Question your boundaries. Underplay your accomplishments. Be nice. Where do we learn this?

✳ Parents/upbringing, even the most well meaning!

✳ Community: programming can start in grade school.

✳ Coaches, teachers, and antimentors, some well meaning, some not so much.

✳ Media, where diminishing messages abound.

✳ Work: damaging external messages can be carried internally like luggage.

✳ Trauma history: this can be the most powerful and hardest to shake.

The frustrating thing is most of us intellectually know we should speak our minds, consequences be damned. Be nice to a beast and you can turn him into a prince? Smile accommodatingly to a boorish boss and maybe he'll change? How backward! We would *never* attempt to do that! And yet deep in our unconscious, these messages still linger, whispering into our collective psyche, causing us to act in ways that run directly counter to our self-interests.

✳ Good little girls don't ruffle feathers.

✳ Good little girls take care of others.

✳ Good little girls make excuses for others' bad behavior.

✳ Good little girls are nice . . . even if that means not being nice to themselves.

✳ Good little girls don't say "no" without apology.

As little girls, we memorized these lessons.

As grown women, we try to reject them.

When we don't succeed, the fallout can be devastating.

Hannah Gadsby, in her mind-blowing stand-up comedy show titled *Nanette*, said it best: "There is nothing more powerful than a broken woman who has rebuilt herself." While I have never felt life has fully broken me, I have had many broken bones along the way. And I treasure each of them. Knowing how to identify and fight against the things that cause us to shut up and step out of our power is one of the most important journeys in our lives. If we avoid delving into them, we stagnate. If we dive in head first, examining, deconstructing, and learning how to ensure we don't let our past dictate our future behavior . . . well, nothing can be more powerful.

Is accommodating, being polite, and prioritizing nice that big of a deal? Yes. Yes, it is. Left unaddressed, we remain forever frozen in time, making choices like chastised little girls rather than grown women. Chastised little girls shrink. Let's be women who know the damaging lessons we have been taught and reject them, claiming space with such ferociousness none would dare try to make us small.

To start with, let's change the thesaurus, shall we?

KIND VERSUS NICE

nice /nīs/

> Pleasant; agreeable; satisfactory.
> "We had a nice time."[1]

kind (kīnd)

> Having or showing a friendly, generous, sympathetic, or warm-hearted nature.
> "Her kind words showed understanding."[2]

These are two common definitions of these words, and most people use them interchangeably. I have found, however, when people describe a "nice" woman to me, they are often describing someone who is agreeable to a fault and subverts her needs for others. When I hear a woman called "kind," she is more likely to be warmhearted in nature but no pushover.

I suggest, as women, we work hard not to be nice. Nice women accommodate others to their own detriment. They don't make waves with their words and avoid words that would label them as difficult. They shrink their power and diminish their opinions. They fall in line. They make themselves small.

As you read this part, read it with the goal of being kind. Let's give each other the benefit of the doubt by being honest with each other and ourselves. Let's be generous, sympathetic, and friendly, but never to someone who diminishes or devalues us. Let's commit to claiming space like kind women who speak our minds, not nice women who shrink to stay safe. And let's never apologize for it.

WHY NOT TO LIE LIKE A SOCIOPATH

Lying is the fast food of communication. It's easy, it's familiar, it feels good in the moment, and it always feels as though there's little cleanup. Even though we have a nagging feeling we shouldn't, we convince ourselves fast food isn't bad for us because, well, everybody's doing it! But, if we partake in too much fast food, it kills us, and similarly, lying slowly kills your soul. Furthermore, look closely. The more powerful a woman is, the less she lies. She has mastered the art of telling the truth.

One of the reasons why I believe we are so tired after work, but suddenly rejuvenated when we talk to family or call a friend, is because sociopathic lying wears us down. Lies are the empty calories of words. They may be food, but they don't really nourish us. Indeed, they are bad for us, and they are especially bad for women.

Lying is self-sabotaging. It is like having a little stone of kryptonite in your pocket. It doesn't kill you right away. It is a slow, imperceptible act of self-sabotage. There is an expectation that women will be caretakers, and that expectation permeates our communication. We are expected to take care of others by prioritizing others' feelings over our truth. One example is the little lies we tell all day to keep things "nice." In the short run, the lies might keep things nice, but they slowly diminish us.

This chapter will teach you *how* to tell the truth—how to stop lying and start living a more truthful life so you can stand by what you believe proudly and without apology. Claim your opinions. Claim your space.

Alternatives to Sociopathic Lying

You can always be honest. Do this by inserting your humanity, and your empathy, into your truth.

PLATITUDES

Greetings

> **Example**: Hi, how are you?
>
> **Replacements**: Hello! Good to see you. Have a good one. Hope you're havin' a good day!
>
> **Example**: I'm fine; how are you?
>
> **Replacements**: Doing well! Gettin' by! You know, it's Monday! Wish it were the weekend! Trying to beat the clock to my meeting!

See No Evil

> **Example**: Beautiful baby! (But still, there's that *rash*!)
>
> **Replacements**: Such a tiny little baby! Oh, she's so little! You're a mom!

It's Too Late

> **Example**: I love your eighties wedding dress!
>
> **Replacements**: That dress is *so* you! That dress makes a real statement!

Or, if asked directly if you like it . . .

> **Replacement**: Well, you know I'm not a huge vintage eighties woman, but I'm not the one getting married! You *own* it, it's *your* day, and girl, I'm *so* happy for you!

NOT SO HARMLESS

The Leadership Lie

> **Example**: It's OK you didn't make it to the potty! Mommy doesn't care! You tried!
>
> **Replacement**: Oops! You missed! Let's clean it up together!

The Condolences Lie

> **Example**: Your pet snake died? What a special snake—I feel so bad for you!
>
> **Replacement**: Your pet snake died! How are you holding up?

The Inspiring Lie

> **Example**: I know we can still win this thing!
>
> **Replacement**: The odds are against us, but I'm not giving up! Never give up!

Lies are a lazy, apathetic communication strategy that sends a clear message: it is not worth my time to care enough to be real with you. While people think this is what they want, on a deep level it obliterates real trust, rendering our fellow human beings invisible. There is nothing worse than that. Nothing. We can't claim space and make others invisible at the same time.

When working to forge real connections, is it possible you will hurt someone's feelings? Yes. Yet someone clumsily, but lovingly, telling us the truth is so much more empowering for us and validating for others than a quick and lazy lie. As long as you apologize and do things differently moving forward, hurt feelings are a small but critical step on the road to real human-to-human connection. Humans *do* want the truth—just kindly delivered. The truth makes us feel seen, heard, and truly connected.

Let's start honoring our truths and caring for each other more. Let's not blow off our fellow human beings less. We don't need to engage in lengthy conversations with each and every human we see. That would be an insane and unworkable time suck. We need only take that extra split second to say the truth to people— to feed them a carrot rather than a greasy, salty, heart-destroying communication french fry.

We can, and should, put a premium on honesty, rather than prepackaged easy lies. Rules are meant to be broken, and some are meant to be discarded altogether. In order to be deemed "appropriate," women should not have to follow the rule that we must diminish our truths and lie like sociopaths. Let's relegate that communication expectation to the trash heap in the sky.

CRAZY FEMINIST BITCH

Platitudes and "harmless" lies are an expectation that women are taught to abide by. They lay the foundation for keeping us small by controlling what we say and ensuring we stay "nice." To be fair, men are expected to do some of that lying as well, just not to the extent that women are. They also receive less pushback if they don't abide by these expectations.

However, there are some communication "rules" women exclusively are expected to follow. If we violate these rules, we receive predictable pushback. We know this intuitively. Most of us consistently adjust our behavior in order to avert the pushback. Consequently, our aversion to pushback keeps us small by controlling what we say and ensuring we stay "nice." Often the pushback comes in the form of very specific words. When we are called these words, we have been trained to believe that we not only must stop advocating for ourselves, but should feel ashamed we ever spoke up in the first place.

If you want to keep a woman small, silence her. If you want to silence her, develop words that are her kryptonite. If she speaks up, call her those words. Use them to shame her. Wield them often enough that she fears if she falls out of line, she will be branded with these words, like a modern-day scarlet letter. Do this, and eventually she will choose silence over speech, qualifiers over statements, and ultimately invisibility over claiming space.

Three Words Used to Keep Us Small

Three words have been used throughout history to keep women quietly in line. The three words are *crazy*, *feminist*, and *bitch*. Each is an effective way to ensure

* Women stuff their anger (crazy).
* Women fear advocating for equal rights (feminist).
* Women fear sharing opinions (bitch).

Let's explore why.

CRAZY

Women are called crazy when we show our anger.

Words under this umbrella: Sensitive/fragile/emotional/hysterical/ hormonal

Message to women: Express your anger and you're an unstable woman who needs to "calm down."

Impact on women: This stigmatizes women's anger. It discourages us from effectively showing a powerful emotion that helps get our point across and can protect us from harm.

Why this really makes no damn sense: When men exhibit this same level of anger, they are, well, angry and usually considered "justified" in their anger. Something is amiss, and it must be rectified!

Why it works anyway: For centuries we have been taught that if we show our displeasure, we will suffer for it.

A hard to believe, and shameful, history of silencing angry women:

Scold's bridle: When women showed displeasure by talking back to their husbands, or complaining to other women if their husbands were beating them, they were punished with a scold's bridle. This device, worthy of any horror movie, was a metal frame that wrapped around the disobedient woman's head and had a bit (some with razor-sharp spikes) that intruded into her mouth like a gag, compressing her tongue. It was used to physically silence women. This device was also used by White people to punish enslaved Black people in America. The history of silencing White women and people of color runs deep.

Isolation: Wealthy White women who sided with the suffragettes were believed to be insane, particularly those who showed their displeasure with being disenfranchised. The cure? Put them alone in a room to rest their brains. Think alone, without your phone, or even a book, in a room. For days. If you were lucky, you could knit! Good times! Read "The Yellow Wallpaper" by Charlotte Perkins Gilman for a fictional account of what this isolation was like.

FEMINIST

Women are called "feminists" when they advocate for equality, justice, and safety individually and collectively.

Words under this umbrella: Lesbian/man-hater/ball breaker/feminazi

Message to women: If you advocate for yourself, or other women, you are a dangerous man-hater, and probably (gasp!) a lesbian.

Impact on women: This implies that women who demand fairness for themselves and each other hate men and are lesbians. These inaccurate and queerphobic sentiments aim to divide us, ultimately weakening our fight for equal justice for all. Demonize the word feminism, and you demonize women fighting for gender equality. In the name of self-interest, they undermine their self-interest.

Why this really makes no damn sense: It always struck me as incredibly illogical that historically "lesbian" and "man-hater" have been conflated. Why would women who spend less time with men than their straight-women counterparts care enough about men to hate them? Feminism is defined by Lexico.com as

> The advocacy of women's rights on the basis of the equality of the sexes.[1]

Advocacy for equality? By that definition, every woman should be a feminist. Indeed, every human should!

Why it works anyway: Equating being a feminist to being a man-hating lesbian will silence women. Straight women taught to fear not being partnered with a man will fear it. What man wants to be with an independent man-hating woman? In addition, as long as being LGBTQ+ continues to be marginalized and targeted, this tactic will work. In certain communities, you need only insinuate a woman is a lesbian, even if she's straight, and she could become a target. If you want to be partnered with a man, best not to advocate for yourself.

A hard to believe, and shameful, history of punishing independent women:

> **Fire:** One of the major reasons women were burned at the stake as witches was because they did not need a man, lived alone, and were financially independent.
>
> **Social stigma:** Being a single woman has carried a social stigma for decades, with labels like "spinster" or "old maid." Women have been taught that if they don't want a man, they will be othered and ostracized, which is far less problematic than burning but still isn't fun.
>
> **Whipping:** In Massachusetts in 1642, Elizabeth Johnson, a maid, was fined and whipped after being caught in the act of having sex with another maid.[2]

Jail: It wasn't until 1961 that Illinois became the first state in America to decriminalize consensual "homosexual" sex.[3]

Violence: According to the FBI, one in five hate crimes involve people in the LGBTQ+ community.[4]

Discrimination: As I write this, half of LGBTQ+ adults live in states where no laws ban job discrimination on the basis of sexual orientation.[5]

Race specific: In the *Code Switch* article "The 'Criminal' Black Lesbian: Where Does This Damaging Stereotype Come From?" author Nicole Pasulka enumerates the incidences of police brutality and other injustices Black lesbians experience.[6]

BITCH

Women are called bitches when they share opinions without apology.

Words under this umbrella: Bossy/abrasive/pushy/aggressive/strident/shrill/nasty

Message to women: If you express your point of view, you are a bitch and you will be silenced.

Impact on women: Shut down a woman's opinions and you shut down her voice. Shut down her voice, and she can't claim space at home or at work. She remains a second-class citizen.

Why this really makes no damn sense: When men express opinions, they are smart, strong, and determined, even about issues they aren't qualified to talk about. For example, strongly arguing about women's experiences. Somehow, this is OK, but when we express pretty much any opinion, we're bitches.

Why it works anyway: Historically, and presently, women with opinions have been punished, both legally and illegally.

A hard to believe, and shameful, history of torture and death for forthright women:

More fire: Women who had opinions, such as midwives, were often targeted as witches and burned at the stake. This practice went on until the mid-seventeenth century.

Beatings: Until the year 1920, when the law changed, women in many states were still allowed to be beaten by their husbands.[7] Their crime? Expressing their opinions, and not necessarily in anger.

Death: Compared to White women, Black and Brown women face even greater consequences for opening their mouths with opinions. For example, when expressing opinions to police, not necessarily in anger, they don't just risk verbal and physical rebukes. They risk death. Black women can die at the hands of law enforcement for saying the same thing a White woman would with little to no pushback. These women have paid the ultimate price for their opinions.

Here are just three examples of the many words commonly combined with race to specifically target women of color:

* Latinx women: fiery Latina (spicy/fiery = angry + crazy)
* African American women: angry Black woman
* Asian women: crazy Asian

Search online for famous women in this category. For kicks, I googled "JLo" and "fiery Latina." I got 411,000 hits. Most were less than kind.

The history of these three words still holds a huge sway in our collective psyche. They still have a clear implication.

You stepped out of line. You will be punished.

We aren't burned at the stake. We aren't silenced with a scold's bridle. But women seen as "angry, crazy feminists" still face massive repercussions.

* **We are less likely to be hired or promoted.** Should we show our opinions without smiles and apologies? We want to, but

we risk being labeled bitches and pushed out of the powerful boys' club.

* **We are less likely to be elected to public office.** Run for office as a self-proclaimed feminist? It's a risk. We will lose voters.

* **We are more likely to face violence.** Openly show our anger when harassed on the street? Probably not; we don't want to be seen as crazy women who need to be shut up.

Just one disheartening example of how powerful these words are can be seen in Hillary Clinton's bid for the presidency.

When Clinton was running against Barack Obama, Glenn Beck famously said this: "When Barack Obama speaks, men hear: 'Take off for the future.' And when Hillary Clinton speaks, men hear, 'Take out the garbage.' . . . She is like the stereotypical bitch, you know what I mean."[8]

Throughout the election, Clinton was called all three words and their subsets. My personal favorites that kept coming up again and again? Nasty, abrasive, shrill, feisty, bossy, bitch, crazy, crazy feminist, and crazy bitch.

Search Engines Reveal Terrifying Truths

Predictably, when you search online for those words with Hillary Clinton's name, the words with the highest hits are "crazy," "feminist," and "bitch."

Then, I got curious. What would happen if I swapped out "Hillary Clinton" with "woman CEO"?

I had predicted "Hillary Clinton bitch" would have many more hits than "woman CEO bitch." I mean, the woman CEOs just were being boss ladies with opinions, overcoming the odds and successfully leading companies, right?

Nope. While Clinton got a ton of hits, women CEOs got way more.

This is not the most scientific study, as many search engines set algorithms to our preferences. That said, I had several friends try this and they all came up with the same order. Try it! I'll put money on "crazy," "feminist," and "bitch" always landing in the top three. (Try it with "woman politician" as well. That will really blow your mind, especially if you combine the three words, such as "woman politician crazy feminist.") I won't give it away. Go try it.

The message to women is clear. Whatever profession you go into, if you become too powerful, you are a crazy feminist bitch and should probably shut up.

Thankfully, women are catching on to why and how these words are used, and many of us are no longer having it.

Remember when Trump said, "such a nasty woman" during a debate with Hillary Clinton? The hashtag #IAmANastyWomanBecause soon went viral. I myself have a mug on my kitchen counter that says, "Nasty Women get stuff done." So many of us now proudly proclaim we are Nasty Women.

Trump may have won the election, but he lost that word. Nasty is ours now. And now let's claim those other words as well!

Claiming Crazy/Feminist/Bitch

My hero Dr. Maya Angelou once said, "I am a feminist. I've been female for a long time now. I'd be stupid not to be on my own side."

We have to stop letting these words be our scold's bridle. Their power needs to be wholly eviscerated.

But can we do it? Can we take these words, neutralize them, and even harness their power to help us claim space? Yes, we most definitely can. Here's how.

DON'T SILENCE OTHER WOMEN.

Never use gender-specific silencing words when referring to other women.

Example: If you think a woman is being "bitchy," ask yourself if the exact same behavior would be acceptable coming from a man.

If the answer is "yes" . . .

Let her speak without shame, and maybe sprinkle in a "That's right! What she said!"

If the answer is "no" . . .

Try a different descriptor. "I feel like you aren't listening to what the team is saying as much as you could," rather than saying, "You know, Jane, you're being a bit of a bitch."

SHUT DOWN SILENCING WORDS.

Never, ever allow these words to stand if you hear someone use them in relation to another woman.

> **Example:** I have a dear friend who has a great response when she hears people refer to women as crazy or bitchy. She says firmly, without apology, "I think you're going to have to use a different word."

> Don't let the word stand.

NEUTRALIZE AND OWN THE WORDS.

Never, ever allow these words to silence *you*. These two strategies work for my clients:

> **Strategy 1: Ask a question.** This is similar to what we would do when encountering any microaggression. "I'm acting crazy? I'm wondering what exactly you mean by that." This will force folks to clarify what they mean. You can then directly address it, rather than letting the word silence you.

> **Strategy 2: *Own it!*** This is what I have found to be most effective, and more empowering. Think Beyoncé, "A diva is a female version of a hustler," or Tina Fey's "Bitches get shit done." Diva used to be something you called women who were being overly demanding. Thanks to women like Beyoncé and Lizzo, it's now a badge of honor. And Tina Fey has done a lot to move the needle on the word bitch.

I believe . . .

* My sons should feel OK being vulnerable.

* Women can run our country as well as men.

* My daughter shouldn't be harassed on the street.

* Women are capable of running Fortune 500 companies.

* Black women should be able to say their opinions just as much as White women.

And I believe every woman has the right to get angry and speak her mind with conviction.

Why? Because I'm a hysterical, strident, shrill, witchy, bitchy, emotional, pushy, abrasive, aggressive, crazy feminist bitch. And proud of it.

In 2020, Representative Alexandria Ocasio-Cortez was accosted on the steps of the Capitol by Congressperson Ted Yoho, who called her a "fucking bitch." She took to the House floor, thanked both Republican and Democratic colleagues for reaching out to her in support, then launched into a speech every human who cares about treating others with respect should watch.

This chapter would not be complete without her response. I encourage you to watch her entire speech.

Here is an edited excerpt:

> I was minding my own business, walking up the steps, and Representative Yoho put his finger in my face; he called me disgusting, he called me crazy, he called me out of my mind, and he called me dangerous.

> Then he took a few more steps and after I had recognized his comments as rude, he walked away and said I'm rude . . .

> I walked inside and cast my vote. I walked back out and there were reporters in the front of the Capitol and in front of reporters Representative Yoho called me, and I quote, "a fucking bitch" . . .

What Mr. Yoho did was give permission to other men . . . to use that language against his wife, his daughters, women in his community, *and I am here to stand up to say that is not acceptable. I do not care what your views are* . . .

Mr. Yoho mentioned that he has a wife and two daughters. I am two years younger than Mr. Yoho's youngest daughter. I am someone's daughter too . . . and *I am here because I have to show my parents that I am their daughter . . . I could not allow that to stand.*[9]

Never, ever let words silence you. Demand more. Get angry. Advocate for a more fair and just world. If anyone has a problem with that, you might suggest they smile pretty, be polite, shut up, and calm down.

Stay loud. Don't apologize. Be 100 percent, and in the immortal words of Lizzo, be "100% that bitch." Here's to crazy feminist bitches. May we be them, raise them, and applaud them.

BOUNDARIES KEEP YOU SAFE

Boundaries. We know they are good for us, but if you don't usually set boundaries, beginning the process can feel a lot like starting to exercise when you're dangerously overweight. Taking the first step is hard. You know you should start but secretly wonder if it really will make much of a difference. You worry folks may say "But that's not you" as you change. And the first few weeks are hell. It's scary, you don't know what you're doing, and it can hurt. However, like working out, once you get into a boundary routine, you'll ask why you didn't a long time ago. Life is just better. Boundaries are hard to establish, but they are life changing! Once you start, I promise the phrase "Please respect my boundaries" will roll off your tongue with confidence, and your life will be better.

Women Need to Stop Apologizing

We apologize when someone bumps into us.

We apologize for claiming *one* armrest.

We apologize when we're interrupted.

We apologize for having an opinion.

We apologize for our appearance.

Women are taught to control how we say things. Women are taught not to demand too much with our words. And women are also taught to apologize for . . . everything. Sometimes we are lying . . . we are just apologizing because we are "expected" to. In reality, we don't feel a damn bit sorry. Sometimes we say we're sorry because we believe that anything but keeping people completely happy all the time deserves an apology.

We apologize with our words, body language, and tone of voice, and we need to stop. We need to stop apologizing.

There are only two times when apologies are OK. Only. Two.

When the request is reasonable, but you just can't do it.

Example: "I'm so sorry I can't help you move even though you helped me. My kid is sick, and I need to stay home with him."

When you have done something wrong.

Example: "I'm sorry I called you a crazy feminist bitch when I was angry at you, and not as a term of endearment. That wasn't cool."

Overapologizing, however, is rampant for women, and it is unnecessary, diminishing, and undermining. You don't have to seek forgiveness or qualify your no. Your firm no is a way of saying, "When you cross a boundary, I will not apologize for erecting it more strongly and without apology."

The following are some alternatives to "I'm sorry!" May they serve as a guide as you break your apology habit. Read on, fierce Wonder Woman, and kick those apologies to the curb.

ALTERNATIVES TO "I'M SORRY!"

In person if it's not a big deal:

Don't say: "Sorry . . . I'm late/the food I made for you is burned/my office is messy."

Do say: "Thanks for . . . waiting/enjoying this slightly burned food/enjoying my cozy office."

In an email if it's not a big deal:

Don't say: "Sorry . . . for the reply all/for the late response."

Do say: "Thanks for your patience with the dreaded reply all/delay."

When stating an opinion:

Don't say: "Sorry . . . but I think [insert your reasonably held position here]."

Do say: Your opinion. (Hint: Start with "I think" or "I believe" and never "I'm sorry.")

When saying no:

Don't say. "So sorry I can't do [insert thing]."

Do say: "[Insert thing] won't work for me. Let's find an alternative that works for both of us?"

To smooth over someone else's faux pas (e.g., someone bumps into you):

Don't say: "Sorry."

Do say: Nothing. (Don't apologize! They should be apologizing to you. Really, they should. They bumped into you.)

When someone has wronged you:

Don't say: "I'm sorry, but you should not have . . . badmouthed me/insulted me/hurt my feelings/violated my space."

Do say: "You should not have . . ." (Kill the sorry. Again, don't apologize for someone else's mistake.)

Apologies are important. Make them count. If you apologize all the time, you're diminishing yourself, and you diminish the credibility of your apologies in situations when they need to count. Apologies actually mean something if used only when needed.

Wonder Woman doesn't walk back to the scene after she has saved hundreds of people, muttering, "Hey, um, sorry about all those parked cars I had to turn over to save you. I realize it's a little messy. I'm really, really sorry." She just feels pretty great for having saved a bunch of people and struts off like a badass. Life is messy. You can't do great things and take great risks if you plan on apologizing for every last thing along the way.

Apologizing for being alive will slowly rob you of your ability to expand into your power. Enough with the apologizing.

Speak your mind without apology. Raise your voice. Don't be sorry.

How to Become a Time Bandit

Traditionally women are told to have an open-door policy about everything and be able to juggle everything. Our time is not valued the same way men's time is. My favorite example of this is when I got hit by a car. For six weeks people came and delivered dinners to my family so my ex-husband wouldn't have to cook. About two weeks after the accident, I was back to light cooking and cleaning, and generally helping him, and yet the meals kept coming to lighten his load and give him more time. When we divorced and I had all of our kids full time, I lost a partner to help me. I was in the same situation he was, arguably worse, because no one was taking the time to do light cooking and cleaning for me. Yet folks expected I would be able to manage this transition. Not one person said, "Wow, you just went from two people running your house to one. You must be taking a lot of time doing housework and cooking. Can I bring you a meal to lighten your load during this transition?" Not. One. Person.

Do I blame them? No, I do not. Not. One. Person. Women are expected to be able to create time to juggle everything. Men are not. This needs to change, and we can begin that process by rejecting that special kind of kryptonite that tells us we can't put down boundaries with our time. How do we do this? We shut the door.

This can be difficult because of . . .

Calls

    Texts

        Emails

            Social media

                Knock! Knock! Knock!

                    KNOCK! KNOCK! KNOCK!

The client who taught me the most about valuing her time and saying no was Samantha, a veritable poster child for being good at just about everything. Samantha was a brilliant woman with thick, curly brown hair, dewy light brown skin, and huge, penetrating light brown eyes. She had an interesting combination of fierce, unwavering conviction and crippling impostor syndrome. After years of hard work, Samantha had finally landed her dream job: chief of staff at an elite university. She was killing it, but the job was killing her.

As a woman of color, Samantha knew she had less room for error than her counterparts. This led her not to delegate a darn thing, which led to her having no time, which led to her doing a shoddy job on a lot of tasks rather than an excellent job on the tasks she had been hired to do. In our first meeting, she laughed her huge, infectious laugh, confessing, "I swear, Eliza, every time my phone beeps I consider taking up day drinking or running over my phone." Then she got serious. "I don't know how long I can keep this up. I'm barely seeing my kids." Samantha had regularly been working fourteen-hour days, doing her job and often the jobs of her staff and her interns. On top of this, the president of the university was constantly texting her, morning, evening, and night, and expected her to be available 24/7.

She was ready to quit.

Samantha and I collaborated and came up with a complex and detailed plan. It failed. Then another. Failed again. Then, after some tweaking, we found a simple three-step plan . . . and it worked! This not only resulted in Samantha liking and thriving in her job again; it also saved her phone . . . and her liver! (OK, knowing Samantha, she wouldn't take up drinking even during the zombie apocalypse, but it did save her mental health.)

I've since taken the blueprint we created and been successfully using it with my other clients. You may read it and say to yourself, "Well, I knew that." You probably do! But are you implementing what you know? Samantha and I found that it wasn't about coming up with a magical plan; it was about acknowledging what the plan was and consistently following through. I suggest you read it, think about what you are and aren't doing, and commit to doing *all* of it. Knowing isn't enough. Doing is what matters. Do, and you will reclaim time.

Three-Step Plan for Creating Time

By me and Samantha, a.k.a. "Samantha the time bandit"

STEP 1: SHUT THE REAL DOOR.
"No, you cannot come in now."

> *If you have an admin* . . . tell your admin that when your door is open, people can come in. When it is not, they may never come in. Try to close it for at least two hours a day.
>
> *If you do not have an admin* . . . talk to your boss and see if she will allow you to implement this policy. Tell her it will optimize your job performance if you work uninterrupted.

STEP 2: SHUT THE CYBER DOOR.
"No, I will not engage with social media all day."

> Once the real door is shut, shut the door to the cyberworld. Put aside at least one hour every day where you do absolutely nothing that requires the internet. This is critically important.

There is plenty you can do without the internet, and you'll do it faster and better if you aren't interrupted. There are apps and software you can use to limit social media time. The technology is constantly evolving. Search online for "10 best apps to reduce social media use" if you need a little extra help and want the latest info.

STEP 3: SHUT DOWN EMAILS.

"No, I will not answer your emails immediately."

This may sound clinically insane/impossible, but research consistently shows you should not respond to emails as they come in but instead attack emails in chunks three to four times a day tops.

You will find that you will not miss anything critical. If it's critical, folks will find a way to reach you, trust me. You many also find, especially on group emails, that if you don't respond, sometimes others will solve the problem themselves without you!

You will also find that you will ultimately have a smaller overall email load. The back and forth can cause unnecessary emailing that starts to resemble texting. I now take this approach, and it saves me about one hour a day.

Make no exceptions unless they are real emergencies, such as your child is ill, the building is on fire, or your favorite musician or movie star randomly shows up requesting a private meeting because they read your fan mail, think you're amazing, and have traveled a treacherous journey with the sole goal of convincing you to run away with them to their private island. Save these three scenarios, do what you need to do to follow through on steps 1–3.

I have a laminated piece of paper in my office that has steps 1–3 on one side and five sentences that help me stick with them on the other. Both sides serve as a little contract with myself to stick with it so I don't start making time-sucking exceptions.

Here are my five:

1. NO! I do not have to do everything, and if things don't turn out as perfectly as if I had done them myself, that's OK.

2. NO! I do not need to answer every email the moment it lands in my inbox.

3. NO! I do not have to be available to all people at all times.

4. NO! I do not need an open-door policy with full access to me at all times.

5. YES! I do have to say no a lot.

I suggest laminating steps 1–3, then really sitting with yourself and deciding what your personal five motivators would be. They may be different from mine. For example, if you have kids, you could write, "I will delegate so I can create time and see my kids more." Find what resonates with you, write it down on the back, and stick it somewhere prominent. The process of really thinking about why you need to do this, and then having those reminders right in front of you, will help you stick to it.

Claim your time. Women who demand that their time be valued have the time and energy to claim more space.

How to Say No: "No" (And Other Suggestions)

It took me a long time to learn to say it, but wow! I really love that word. If you don't love it, now's your moment to fall in *love*!

It's a beautiful little word. It needs *no* explanation. You are never obligated to apologize or be sorry about it. It packs a hell of a punch. And don't let anyone fool you—saying no isn't being mean. It's putting down a boundary, and putting down boundaries is a great way to claim space!

I shall leave you with examples of that beautiful two-letter word.

As with sorry, there are times for softening your no with a gentle, kind word—for example, "No, I can't go on a girls' vacation with you. I really, really want to, but I have a huge work deadline." Or, immediately after you break up with someone, in the same conversation, "No. I'm not going to change my mind about breaking up with you. I understand how hard this is. It's hard for me. You're a wonderful person and I hope we can be friends, but I just can't date someone who [insert your personal deal breaker here]." You don't have to justify it—*it's your deal breaker.*

That said, there are many times we say we're sorry when saying no with a simple, firm "no" would do. Here are some handy examples:

Person: *"It's more convenient for me if I talk to you about this minor issue during your no-office-hours time. Can I just pop by for about twenty minutes?"*

You: "No."

Optional unapologetic follow-up: "You have asked me this before, and the answer is still no. Please don't ask again for minor issues."

Person: *"I know you have never, ever wanted our sex life to involve [insert sex thing that just isn't your thing—you don't have to qualify. It's not your thing.]. But that seems really uptight. Can we please do it anyway?"*

You: "No."

Optional unapologetic follow-up: "And if you continue to ask me to do something sexually I don't want to do, I'm out."

Person: *"I know you have never, ever wanted our sex life not to involve [insert sex thing that really is your thing—you don't have to qualify. It's your thing.]. But that seems really slutty. Aren't you ashamed of yourself?"*

You: "No."

Optional unapologetic follow-up: "I know this isn't your thing, and of course we will never do anything we both don't really want to do, but if you continue to shame me about my preferences around sex, I'm out."

Person: *"I know you said you are on a deadline and absolutely can't be disturbed unless the building is on fire, but can I interrupt for just a second?"*

You: "No."

Optional unapologetic follow-up: "As I said, I have to get this done."

Person: *"If you were nice, you would put up with my crappy behavior."*

You: "No."

Optional unapologetic follow-up: "There is nothing mean about me asking you to stop [insert behavior that is crappy]."

Person: *"I think you don't understand [insert your area of subject matter expertise here]. Can't I explain it to you?"*

You: "No."

Optional unapologetic follow-up: "That's my subject matter expertise. I don't need you, who does not study this, to explain it to me."

Person: *"Why do you have to act so crazy? Come on! You really don't like me saying that skirt really shows off your legs?"*

You: "No."

Optional unapologetic follow-up: "Stop commenting on my body. You're my boss, not my partner."

(White) Person: *"Can I touch your hair?"*

(BIPOC) You: "No."

Optional unapologetic follow-up: "Don't ask again."

Person: *"Why don't you relax, chill out, and calm down?"*

You: "No, No, and No."

Optional unapologetic follow-up: "And I think you might want to examine that my voice isn't raised, yours is, and you're telling me to calm down."

Person: *"Well, could you at least stop being such a crazy feminist bitch?"*

You: "No. Not now. Not ever."

Optional unapologetic somewhat wordy but delicious follow-up: In 1918 Rebecca West wrote, "I myself have never been able to find out precisely what feminism is: I only know that people call me a feminist whenever I express sentiments that differentiate me from a doormat." I am not a doormat. I am, however, a crazy feminist bitch. Thanks for the compliment.

Figure out when it's hardest for you to say no. Write these scenarios down. Practice saying no and without apology. Come up with your own unapologetic follow-ups. They don't have to be as snarky as mine. I had a little too much fun with this section.

Say yes to no.

Happy no-ing.

PART 4

CLAIM SAFETY IN ANY SPACE

Shut It Down!

Stop aggressors and protect yourself!

Justice is about making sure that being polite is not the same thing as being quiet. In fact, often times, the most righteous thing you can do is shake the table.

—CONGRESSWOMAN ALEXANDRIA OCASIO-CORTEZ

In third grade I had an unrequited crush on a dreamy little boy named Isiah. I was absolutely certain I would marry him when I grew up! One day out of the blue, Isiah blurted out, "Eliza! You're *so* pretty!" He then promptly hauled off and hit me, hard, *really* hard. I immediately started running to his house, tears streaming down my cheeks and absolutely determined to get him grounded for life.

When I reached the porch, my now *not* future mother-in-law, Bema, was waiting, a look of profound concern on her face. "What's wrong, Eliza? Are you hurt?"

"*Yes!* Isiah hit me on the shoulder—*really hard!* It *still hurts!*" By this time Isiah was standing next to me, breathless, ready to make his case.

He didn't have to.

To my shock, his mom looked relieved, then laughed warmly and said, "Oh, Eliza, don't make him feel too bad about it. He hit you because he likes you, right, Isiah?" Isiah looked a little surprised, but then relieved. His mom looked at him with sympathy, as if he was the most endearing child she had ever met.

"It's OK, Isiah." She smiled, comforting him.

At first, I felt deeply, profoundly confused. Then I stopped thinking about my shoulder, which still hurt. I pushed my anger aside, ignoring that voice in my head that said, "But Eliza! You *know* this is *not* right." I absorbed my new normal.

I guess it was *good* he hit me. It meant he liked me.

This is my story, and I'm pretty confident you have one like it. It's a story as old as time.

Little girls learn a powerful lesson from these stories: the world is unsafe for you, and that's OK. *Learn to live with it, work to accommodate it, and sometimes don't only justify it but embrace it.* It's OK for a boy to hit a girl, but only if he likes you. Push your own pain aside. Forgive, sympathize, and appreciate men who can't express their feelings except through violence.

Violence = Love

Be nice. Be polite. And be thankful you are loved at all.

As little girls we learn quickly we do not have the right to exist safely in any space, sometimes even with the people who profess to care about us. We teach little girls the safety scale, a scale that dictates where we go, what we do, and how we live. When entering a space, we quickly place ourselves on the scale. How safe, or unsafe, are we? The safety scale is so woven into the fabric of our history and training that most of us don't know we have it, much less that it can play a huge role in dictating our behavior.

The safety scale slides from total emotional safety to dire physical danger. Both extremes are rare, although they are more common for women in targeted groups. All of us, however, live much of our lives navigating the complex and sometimes terrifying realities of everything in between.

Emotional Safety

How emotionally safe is this space?

Is there a dangerous group dynamic?

Is there a particular person I need to carefully navigate?

Is this a "big blow up" danger or a "death by a thousand cuts" situation?

Sitting down in an airplane, a man spreads out, taking both armrests. You make an assessment with lightning speed. "If I push my arm onto the armrest, is it safe? Will I face fallout? Will he get annoyed? Become angry? Will he think I'm flirting? Will he even care?" Just how safe are you to claim the space you rightfully deserve?

Physical Danger

On the other side of the spectrum are the big scary space stealers. The things that conjure up images of boogeymen jumping out of bushes, threatening our physical safety.

Is this space safe enough to be in at all?

If I shouldn't be here, can I leave safely?

Do I need a male protector in this space?

Is it worth being in the space if I need a male protector?

What precautions must I take to mitigate my risk?

Walk to your car alone at night from a restaurant, and that boogeyman looms large. You know a shortcut, but the street is dark and unpopulated. No. That space is not safe for you. You cannot claim it. So you go the long route and for good measure call a friend because that seems to deter run-of-the-mill harassers. If you can't get someone on the phone, you pretend you're on the phone—it makes an unsafe space feel just a little safer. This is an issue women face throughout our lives, and it's far more common than most of our male counterparts understand. I recently told my friend Alek that there are apps women use so their friends can track them and call 911 if necessary. The fact apps like that exist says a lot. The fact Alek, an enlightened intersectional feminist male ally, had no idea these exist shows the two worlds women and men live in.

The right to feel safe and secure in a space should be a fundamental human right. Yet for women, that right is rarely fulfilled. Often we live in a state of hypervigilance, navigating the best we can around unsafe people and institutions.

It's also critical to note that White women and Black women have a different experience with space.

Dr. Nia Nunn is a professor, researcher, and community leader who has created transformative antiracist modules, workshops, and talks to educate White people and empower and uplift the voices of young people, particularly Black women and girls. I also am very lucky to call Dr. Nunn a mentor on issues of race and equally lucky to call her my friend. Dr. Nunn has spoken with me at great length about issues of Blackness, "spaciality," and Black womanhood. She pointed out to me that when White women walk into a space, it is being a woman that puts us in danger, but when Black women walk into a space, the experience is quite different.

"A student of mine described it perfectly," said Dr. Nunn. "She said 'My Blackness enters the space before I do' when describing the challenge of navigating predominantly White spaces."[1]

For women of color, there is an extra layer of what does and does not make a space unsafe. I will address this layer in depth, with the help of Dr. Nunn, in the final part.

This part will teach you three critical skills:

1. **Finding your center.** Embrace your reality and know your value in a world that can undermine both.

2. **Identifying different threats.** Dissect, and name, the different challenges you face so you can better combat them.

3. **Neutralizing unsafe environments.** Implement strategies to optimize your safety without making yourself invisible.

I faced a philosophical conundrum when approaching this section. This part is about behaviors of others that make us feel unsafe. We do not do this to ourselves. So the question is this: If a woman is walking down the street and men are catcalling her, what should I do? Teach the woman how to handle catcalling? Perhaps. I would argue there is a fairer solution: teach men to self-reflect so they stop catcalling. Writing this part felt a bit like telling women it is women, and not men, who are responsible for managing men's poor behavior. On top of this, many of the solutions historically offered to women may have made them safe but were incredibly damaging. Don't want to be seen as a bitch? Offer fewer opinions and smile more. Want to feel safe from assault? Try not to dress like a "slut." These victim-blaming solutions are psychologically damaging and diminish us. They tell us the solution to feeling unsafe claiming space is to make ourselves smaller. When we feel diminished, we feel less powerful. When we feel less powerful, we are less safe. When facing these challenges, we must not shrink; we must expand into our power. This part will give you powerful techniques to do that.

Keep Me Blind, Keep Me Small

Claiming space is a hell of a lot harder than simply calling out the behavior. "Hey, if you could please stop [insert bad behavior], that would be just lovely!" seems like it should work. It often doesn't. When we call out certain behaviors, the following can happen, in this order:

1. **Denial.** They refuse to see their own behavior.

   Man: "What are you talking about? I never did that!"

2. **Blame shifting.** If denial doesn't work, they shift the blame, insinuating it isn't their behavior that's a problem—it's the woman's mental state.

   Man: "Calm down and stop being so crazy/bitchy."

3. **Gaslighting.** The woman begins to doubt herself because she's been convinced that what happened didn't actually happen, or at least it didn't happen the way she experienced it.

   Woman: "Maybe I *am* crazy?"

4. **Blindness.** The woman begins to distrust her compass, questioning if she's seeing the man's behavior clearly.

   Woman: "Maybe it *wasn't* that big a deal. Maybe I *made it up*. Or *it's my fault*."

Once stages 3 and 4 are reached, neutralizing behaviors becomes close to impossible. *If you cease to believe yourself, if you no longer see something clearly, stopping it can be extraordinarily difficult.* Without the right tools, this is true even if you're a committed space claimer. The crazy-making pushback we experience from calling out a behavior can be more unsettling than the behavior itself.

You will learn techniques to shut down behaviors in these chapters, but you will also learn to mitigate pushback you may get when you claim space in unsafe spaces. I have read many articles and books that blithely tell women to shut down behaviors without any understanding of potential fallout, or tools to circumvent said fallout. The chapters in this part will do both.

I believe both women and men, even the men who engage in this behavior the most, have little kids who live inside them who are crying out, "But Isiah! But Eliza! You both *know* this is *not* right." Yet so much of society tells us to ignore that moral compass crying out for change. And so many of us gamely go along with this destructive narrative. We don't have to.

We must reject the upside-down messages we have been told time and time again. Until every one of us is safe to speak our truths and walk with confidence in any space, none of us are safe. We must fight tooth and nail to claim our space however and wherever we can.

The little girls in us still remember what it felt like to believe we deserved better. Those little girls expected to become women who lived in a fair and safe world. They remember the painful and confusing mental gymnastics it took to accept the world as it is. The little girl in each of us still tells us that this is not right, that we deserve better, so much better. Let's do right by them.

FIND YOUR COMPASS

The first step to combating unsafe spaces is believing yourself. You would think that this would be easy. Either we feel unsafe or we don't, right? Nope. Not for many of us!

Even if your conscious doesn't know if you are unsafe, your unconscious always does. If you consciously feel unsafe, you can mindfully respond to this feeling. If you don't, you unconsciously will employ *all kinds of tactics in response to your lack of safety, many of which are wildly counterproductive.*

We can give up our space because we are forced to, or we can give it up because we have been so strongly trained to see our shrunken selves as normal. That is our emotional kryptonite. The first way to combat this is to begin to tune in to what my ever brilliant, wise friend, Kim Munson-Burke, calls our compass.

What is your compass? Is it your soul? Your intellect? Everything you have been taught by the smartest mentors in your life? By watching a lot of *Star Wars*? Does love, in all its forms, guide our choices? Truth is, I don't know. I just know it exists, that women have it turned sideways at a young age (some more than others) and that the more we right it as adults, the safer we are.

Safe women claim space better. It's hard to claim space when you're shrinking in fear.

Although a compass can't be defined, it can be explained. It all goes back to Uncle Bob.

Remember when you were little and you didn't want to give Uncle Bob a kiss at Christmas dinner? Remember your parents' reaction? Embarrassed apologies to Uncle Bob. Then your parents turned to you with disappointed, forced smiles. "Come on, be a good girl. Give Uncle Bob a hug and a kiss!" And you did. You gave him a hug and a kiss even though you really didn't want to.

OK, maybe that didn't happen to you, but we all had things like that happen. Moments when a voice inside us conveyed a clear message, and we were told to ignore that voice.

Now in Uncle Bob's defense, I'm not saying he's a creepy child molester. Who knows *why* you didn't want to kiss and hug him. Maybe he *was* creepy and he scared you. Maybe his shirt smelled bad. Maybe he had a huge booger hanging precariously out of his veiny nose. Or maybe, just maybe, there was no tangible reason . . . maybe *you just didn't want to* . . . and yet in the end, you did what you were told. And that's when you started to lose touch with your compass.

Years later you walked into an office. The man interviewing you put his hand on the middle of your back then slid his hand down, guiding you into your chair by the small of your back. "Well, that's really not OK!" your compass screamed. (Or perhaps "Punch him! Now! Or at least don't work here!") That's when you make *the mistake*, the one you've been taught to make. You unclench your fists, looking around the room for a "reality check." Hmmmm. No one else seemed to think this was a problem. You tell the voice in your head she's nuts. It must be you. This must be OK. Then you smile at your future creepy-as-hell boss and walk down the road to a very unpleasant stint at a new job you never should have taken. You kiss Uncle Bob.

When we weren't believed, when we were undermined or diminished, when we were rewarded for denying our reality, praised for submitting to the rules of the powerful . . . all of these moments began the process of letting others define our reality for us. That's when phrases like "Did that just happen?" or "Does that seem right to you?" or "Am I crazy?" started creeping into our vocabulary.

Even if you had the most validating upbringing and happened to avoid 99 percent of the sexism out there, the world we live in makes listening to our compass a challenge. Why? Power structures set reality with what I call the "This makes no sense . . . but OK" rules of life.

Some examples, at the time of this writing:

* White women still get paid 79 cents to men's dollar, and it's lower for women of color.[1] And somehow every woman in the US isn't rallying in the streets. Makes no sense, but OK.

* Almost half of all murders of women in this country are by current or former intimate partners.[2] And yet domestic violence isn't considered as much of a threat to the people in our country as terrorism. Makes no sense, but OK.

* Our daughters have to cover their drinks when out in bars for fear of being drugged.[3] Makes no sense, but OK.

* A man who said he liked to grab women by their genitalia without "asking" (which is, you know, a crime) was elected president. Makes no sense, but OK.

* We are told to kiss Uncle Bob, even when we clearly don't feel comfortable pressing our lips to this particular man's cheek at the moment. Makes no sense, but OK.

The only way to accept something that makes zero sense is to ignore the fact that it makes zero sense. This is highly problematic. When you stop listening to your gut telling you "Something is seriously not OK here," all your decision-making processes are undermined. This is when you start looking to others to make decisions for you. But here's the thing . . .

You can't steer your ship with the rudder on another person's boat. Sooner or later, and probably sooner, you will lose your way.

Reclaim Your Compass

So, how do you get your compass back? How do you find that voice that tells you "I know what I feel. I know what I should do. I'm going to do it, and without apology or anyone else's permission"?

There are two steps. If the first doesn't work, go to step 2.

STEP 1: CHECK IN WITH YOUR GUT

Trust that you know the answer, and it's the right one.

If a space feels unsafe, it is. You know the answer.

If you don't trust someone, they are untrustworthy. You know the answer.

If you feel your boundaries are being crossed, they are. You know the answer.

If you think that person is being a total jerk to that Black woman checking people out at the grocery store even though everyone around you doesn't seem to notice or care, you're right. You should intervene. You know the damn answer.

Think of it like the advice they give you before you take the SATs—always go with your first answer. Am I saying you should never think things out, weighing pros and cons? Absolutely not. But that's not what a compass is there for. A compass is there for decisions that are too intangible to quantify. We ignore our compass at our peril.

STEP 2: WHEN YOUR GUT FAILS YOU

Sometimes, however, we just can't tell what we are feeling or thinking. This is especially true when our safety scale isn't at the physical danger extreme. It's when we are feeling emotionally unsafe and start convincing ourselves it's all in our heads or we aren't justified. "Go ahead, kiss Uncle Bob!" rings in our ears during these moments. When this happens, I find women can almost always reconnect with their truth by using that handy tip from chapter 4—flipping the script. This simply means asking yourself to reverse the situation:

1. Would a man be treated this way?

2. If he were treated this way, would he tolerate the behavior?

3. If he would not, would he demand he be treated fairly?

4. If the answer is yes, you damn well have the right to do the same or do something to right the situation!

Here's an example of how it works in this context.

Last fall I called Yvette, a community leader, public servant, and dear friend, to see if she might endorse Amelia, a highly qualified candidate I was supporting.

Yvette sighed. She was torn. She had been contacted by Sam, Amelia's top competition. Sam begged her not to endorse Amelia. When she pushed back, he pushed back harder. Indeed, he would not get off the phone until Yvette grudgingly committed to at least considering not endorsing Amelia.

I paused for a second, then said to her, "Do you think Amelia would've called you and pushed you like that not to endorse Sam?" Yvette didn't pause for a moment. "Absolutely not." Then I asked if she would've called Sam, had the shoe been on the other foot, and pushed so hard. She burst out laughing. "A Black woman calling a White man and telling him who to, and not to, endorse?! I'd be *that* angry Black woman!" No way in any universe would Yvette ever do that.

We then commiserated about the fact that Yvette, who is an absolutely brilliant and aware woman and takes no crap from anybody, had felt uncomfortable with the interaction but wasn't exactly sure if she was justified. Sam had acted as if he would be the victim of Yvette, should she endorse the candidate of her choice, and a part of her bought it. After our conversation, Yvette decided to endorse Amelia. She would not ever ask Sam to refrain from endorsing somebody, so why should she not expect the same courtesy from him? It took Yvette flipping the script for her to get the clarity she needed about how out of line Sam had been.

This concept holds true for microaggressions. It holds true for sexual harassment. It holds true for being passed over for a raise. It holds true for mansplaining and manspreading and all of those indignities women face. We live our lives realizing we will be confronted, every day, with behaviors that make us feel unsafe. In order to survive, we push that SNR feeling away. (SNR stands for something's not right—a term coined by my sister-from-another-mother, Katie Spallone.) We push through and ignore what's happening for the sake of harmony, or making someone comfortable, or averting pushback. In some ways this is a good tactic. If we noticed every single moment where people made us feel unsafe in a space, we would probably not be able to function. That said, we must not lower the bar so much that we don't take steps needed to make ourselves feel safe, as is our right.

What I do know is when I have a confused feeling, it's because I ignored that wisdom and I didn't trust myself. When I trust myself, the results are usually good.

Listen to your compass, and if you can't find it, flip the script.

You never have to kiss Uncle Bob. Not ever.

A Note on Physical Safety

Most of the chapters in this section address feeling emotionally unsafe in a space. Many of us already know what to do when we feel physically unsafe: get out of there as fast and safely as we can. For those fortunate women who have not experienced a great deal of trauma, your compass is intact and you know what to do when confronted with physical danger.

Many women, however, have a history of trauma, and it can be hard to know what feels unsafe. Some women who have been assaulted will put themselves back in dangerous situations, similar to that which originally caused trauma, in order to regain control over their sexuality. This often results in being traumatized again, creating a horrific cycle of abuse. If you feel you don't always know when you are and are not safe, it is imperative you seek therapy from a licensed therapist who does work in trauma. There are also some helpful books on trauma, including *The Body Keeps the Score: Brain, Mind, and Body in the Healing of Trauma* by Bessel van der Kolk.

Most of the chapters in this part will address more subtle, insidious situations where we are unsafe, and how to combat them. Given that the next chapter is about physical and emotional bullying and sexual harassment, you may be thinking, "Subtle? Really?" Yes. We are so accustomed to kissing Uncle Bob that it can be hard to identify what is or is not a safe space.

ANGER, BULLYING, SEXUAL HARASSMENT

One great way to get in touch with our compass is by giving ourselves permission to get angry. Not annoyed. Not bothered. Not frustrated. *Angry, furious, rageful, and pissed off!* If you feel like, "Oh no, people will call me nuts if I act that way," please refer back to the chapter on being a crazy feminist bitch for a refresher.

Women's anger is mighty and it is powerful, yet we are told to hide it, push it away, or deny it.

We need to embrace our anger. It is there to guide us, to help us listen to the SNR feeling. A world of women unafraid of their anger is a world of women ready to insist they be treated with dignity and respect, always.

As Audre Lorde famously said, "Your silence will not protect you." The flip side of that quote is this: Your anger will protect you. Indeed, it will protect you when you need it most.

Anger inoculates women against shrinking and fuels our expansion.

This chapter is about bullying and sexual harassment. But more importantly, it's about women's anger, and how that anger can help protect us when we feel unsafe in a space.

Remember in the beginning of the book when I asked the question about why one woman could sit in a coffee shop without harassment while another had to manage man after man coming over to her, refusing to leave her alone? The woman who sat undisturbed was in touch with her anger. She might as well have had a sign on her forehead that proclaimed, "I'd like to read the paper in peace. Kindly do not mess with me."

People felt her power and didn't dare bother her.

The more women have access to their anger, the stronger they become at maintaining their limits and, in turn, the more powerful they become. They emanate that power. These women are top-shelf space claimers. We can all become these women.

I sought out an expert on the subject of bullying, Dr. Kiranjit Bali.[1] I'm incredibly fortunate to know many warmhearted, thoughtful, and brilliant women. I'm proud to say Dr. Bali, who I know as Kiran, is one of them. She is a licensed mental health counselor in the state of New York and also has a doctoral degree in criminal justice, specifically in the area of victimology. Her research focuses on workplace bullying in higher education and its impact.

Let's start with how Kiran explained the relationship between sexual harassment and bullying. To start with, according to the United States Equal Employment Opportunity Commission (EEOC), this is the basic definition of sexual harassment:

> Unwelcome sexual advances, requests for sexual favors, and other verbal or physical conduct of a sexual nature

constitutes sexual harassment when submission to or rejection of this conduct explicitly or implicitly affects an individual's employment, unreasonably interferes with an individual's work performance or creates an intimidating, hostile or offensive work environment.[2]

In short, it is sexually inappropriate behavior at work that makes you miserable. While some people see sexual harassment as an entirely different category from bullying, Kiran explained to me that, indeed, sexual harassment can be seen as a subset of bullying, but there are some critical differences.

Here is what sets sexual harassment apart from other kinds of bullying:

1. Our culture is steeped in shame and humiliation around issues of sexuality.

2. Therefore, women often feel ashamed and embarrassed when sexually harassed.

3. This results in internalized negative rather than legitimately negative feelings toward the harasser or a fear of public shaming.

4. The woman is silenced.

This sequence is a predictable and powerful tool of oppression.

Despite these differences, we can employ the same techniques to put the kibosh on sexual harassment and bullying, as both are fundamentally issues of power and abuse of power.

So What Is Bullying?

Bullying is a power imbalance. The person who is being bullied/victimized can't defend themselves. They either don't know how or are defenseless against the bully. According to Kiran, "Women are punished for using the behaviors men do, so they often get targeted more and therefore bullied more." Bullying isn't just pushing people or yelling at them. There are many different ways to bully, which is why it can be so tough to see and identify.

Flavors of bullying:[3]

PASSIVE VERSUS ACTIVE

Passive: silent treatment/insinuations

Active: direct aggressive confrontation

NONVERBAL VERSUS VERBAL

Nonverbal: hitting/pushing

Verbal: chastising, yelling

INDIRECT VERSUS DIRECT

Indirect: gossip, encouraging others to bully for you

Direct: doing the bullying yourself

How Do I Know if I've Been Targeted by a Bully?

The following are several ways to identify if you have been the target of bullying. (If your organization would like to deep dive into workplace bullying, check out this resource by the researchers who helped me create the following arrow: *Bullying and Harassment in the Workplace. Theory, Research and Practice.*)[4]

If several of these words jump to mind when you think of someone, you may have been the target of bullying.[5]

Critical

    Coercing

        Devaluing

            Gossiping

                Accusatory

                    Malevolent

                        Humiliating

                            Intimidating

                                Domineering

If several of these *actions* jump to mind, they most definitely have targeted you:

                                Demeaning

                        Micromanaging

                Giving the silent treatment

            Aggressive finger pointing

          Assigning undoable tasks

        Shoving and blocking

      Threatening violence

    Spreading gossip

Shouting in rage

So What Are You Going to Do about It?

This brings me back to anger. When we are bullied, it is a normal reaction to get angry. So often, we do not. We are trained to be nice (there's that horrible word again!), smooth things over, not tackle things head on, but instead use lots of qualifiers and smile while we're at it.

Unfortunately, our unconscious doesn't like when we ignore our anger, and our anger doesn't go away just because we tamp it down. We simply internalize our anger. That's when things don't go well.

There are two kinds of anger, ineffective internalized anger and effective externalized anger. One works; one doesn't. I'll start with what won't work.

Ineffective internalized anger or, more bluntly, different ways to stuff your anger:[6]

* **Exit: we leave physically/emotionally.** We leave the situation or internally shut down. I know too many clients who have walked away from great jobs because they simply could not tolerate the bullying any longer. The bully wins big time in this scenario.

* **Loyalty: we kiss ass.** I see this as the most insidious. If you've ever seen a woman at work get bullied by her boss and try to shut it down by working harder to please, that's this phenomenon. It's painful to watch and flings the door wide open for more bullying. I've done this. I think most of us have.

* **Neglect: we drag our feet by accident on purpose.** You just start doing a crappy job and ignoring work in order to signal your displeasure. This doesn't work. Indeed, instead of creating change, you will probably just get fired.

* **Cynicism: we get negative.** This involves adopting a cynical attitude. "Work will always be awful" or "Relationships will always be awful." This is a great way to create a self-fulfilling prophecy.

* **Pleading: "please, please stop!"** This involves crying or getting teary and begging the bully to stop. This is a genuine and legitimate reaction, and sadly it won't change the bully. Actually, it will probably embolden him.

Stuffing your anger does not work. It can ultimately lead to depression, anxiety, eating disorders, self-injury, and even thoughts of suicide. So what's the solution? You guessed it! Get. Angry.

Effective Externalized Anger

By Kiran and Eliza

The following are the steps to combating bullying, and they all come down to *anger*!

IDENTIFY WHEN YOU ARE ANGRY

This can be very hard because women spend a lot of time rationalizing away our anger. This makes sense. Anger isn't always safe for us. But as we've seen, stuffing it is, in the long run, a hell of a lot less safe.

* **Know your limit.** Let your anger tell you if a limit has been crossed. Think "Oh, I've hit my limit. I'm too angry for this to continue." Start to check in with your compass. I often have clients and students rank their feelings all day long on a scale of 1–10. Number 1 is "Golly, I'm mildly annoyed I dropped that" and 10 is "If I could kill that asshole, I would!" People are consistently astounded by how much angrier they are during the day than they thought they were! We then look at the list, and most clients discover that anything over a 3 is not OK with them. Learn your own scale. Hint: Given how much women are taught to diminish anger, if you feel more than a little annoyed, you are probably furious. If you are furious, whatever is happening is not OK.

✳ **Name that boundary!** Name the boundary for what it is—for example, "This is gaslighting" or "This is the silent treatment." Use the previous list of ways to identify bullying to help you pinpoint what is going on.

✳ **Prepare for pushback.** Understand the pushback you might get and prepare for it, big or small. Realize, at worst, you might have to leave your relationship or your job.

✳ **Pep talk.** Tell yourself you have the right to have the boundary. "This person is gaslighting me. I don't want to argue my reality over and over anymore."

✳ **Say it: use your anger, and show it!** State your boundary to the bully, with anger. "I told you not to borrow money off my desk without asking, and you did it again. Now you're telling me I said it was OK. I never said that. I'm angry. You knew not to do this. Don't appropriate my stuff again. Respect my space. And yeah, I need my twenty bucks back. Now."

Pro tip: *Do not* water down the words "angry/mad/furious" by swapping with "annoyed/upset/bothered." Tell it like it is. You are angry. Own it. The most effective way to show anger is with high-playing behaviors. This shows that not only are you angry but you know how to control it and harness it to make your point crystal clear. It also shows you do not fear your anger but embrace it. And a woman who embraces her anger is not to be trifled with.

Now, as you're reading this you may be thinking, "OMG, the *pushback* I would get! " You are absolutely right. You may get pushback in the form of new bullying tactics, such as the bully saying you are overreacting, crazy, or victimizing them. The bully might give you the silent treatment or yell at you. Use your anger to meet their anger. You have a right to your opinions and a right to your anger. Stand firm. Stay angry. This does not mean screaming and yelling, although that's not the worst thing ever. It means telling people you are angry and you will no longer tolerate their behavior. Tap into your anger to fuel your courage and determination to face the bully.

In some situations the power dynamic is so disproportionate that we can't leave a relationship or a job, at least not right away. This is real. I asked Kiran what she does with clients when this happens. She said she encourages her client to start building up her independence and options *while still in the situation* so eventually she can leave safely. Here are ways you can do that.

Prepare to Get Out: Building Your Independence

The following are suggestions for shoring up your situation:

1. **Discover.** Discover and build up new talents and skills. Take classes, get a part-time job, start a small business, start looking for a new job. Doing any of these things while still in a financially secure situation is easier than on your own, especially if you have kids.

2. **Fortify.** Shore up your network, as we talked about in chapter 6. See how much your friends can support you, whether this means taking you out to dinner or letting you stay with them while you get your feet on the ground.

3. **Ask.** If you have a family with financial resources who are willing to help you, get specific about how much they would be willing to help once you leave. Be very concrete about your ask. I was married to a doctor prior to getting divorced. I was fortunate. My family was able and willing to spot me the down payment on the lawyer. It made all the difference.

Once you have shored up your situation, two things will happen:

1. You will leave, and you will be better off.

    or

2. Your situation will get better. (On rare occasions women find once they have the ability to leave, they are much more able to

stand up for themselves effectively. The bullying stops, and the situation gets better.)

Bullies smell our weakness, but bullies also fear our anger.

Women's anger is our emotional canary in the coal mine. It's our clue that, as my friend Katie says, things are SNR. It's uniquely ours, and as the many angry women telling their stories during the #MeToo movement showed us, women claiming space with women's anger can fuel bloodless revolutions.

My favorite book in the world is still a book written by Madeleine L'Engle for young people, *A Wrinkle in Time*. When I was younger, I loved this book because, fundamentally, it's about the power of love. I believed, and still do believe, that love is the most powerful force in the universe. That said, I also believe in the power of anger, and as an adult, I understand the book was also about teaching little girls that it's OK to be angry. If you find yourself being bullied, I hope this quote from the book helps you to claim space, with anger, even if you are afraid.

> "Stay angry, little Meg," Mrs Whatsit whispered. "You will need all your anger now."

MICRO-AGGRESSIONS

Bit by bit, microaggressions will erode a piece of your soul . . . not a huge piece, but a piece. Rarely do people attempt to take power from you in a big, noticeable chunk. They start slowly and gently, often with a smile. You barely know it's happening. They may exhibit a warm, friendly behavior while they grab just a tiny bit from you. You feel a little prick and wonder, "Did that just happen?" Then you dismiss it. Then it happens again. Peck after peck. You didn't feel anything. You must be overreacting. Maybe you imagined it. Then slowly, ever so slowly, you begin to realize something is wrong. You can't put your finger on it, but you feel your personhood being eroded. If you remain unaware, microaggressions can destroy you bit by bit, like a frog in a pot of heating water. Once you can see them, you can neutralize them.

How Power Is Taken

There is a word for that peck, peck, peck . . . microaggressions.

Here is the academic definition of microaggressions:

> The everyday verbal, nonverbal, and environmental slights, snubs, or insults, whether intentional or unintentional, that communicate hostile, derogatory, or negative messages to target persons based solely upon their marginalized group membership.[1]

It's easy to look at someone with a pointy white hat burning a cross on someone's lawn and say, "That person's a racist." It's easy to hear a man say, "You know, you should be barefoot and in the kitchen," and realize that man is pretty damn sexist. Sadly, people have gotten much better at subtle, hard-to-pin-down "isms." I have deemed this damaging antihero superpower "top-shelf sexism" or "top-shelf racism."

According to the 2007 *American Psychologist* article "Racial Microaggressions in Everyday Life," there are three categories of microaggressions: microassault, microinvalidation, and microinsult.[2] Understanding them can help you identify them if you are a target, or help you stop doing them inadvertently yourself.

* **Microassaults (often conscious).** These are "explicit violent verbal or nonverbal attacks meant to hurt the intended victim through name-calling, avoidant behavior or purposeful discriminatory actions."

  Example: At Cornell, students of color I have mentored from the Latinx dorm reported White students often tell hurtful "jokes" about immigrants when they are around. These are microassaults, and these students are intending to cause harm.

* **Microinvalidations (often unconscious).** "Verbal comments or behaviors that negate, or nullify [someone's] psychological thoughts, feelings or experiences." (In other words, what's happening to you isn't really happening. It's in your head.)

  Example: A White female client of mine was constantly interrupted when she spoke at meetings in which she was the only woman. Eventually she quietly said at a meeting, "Hey guys, could you let me finish?" They immediately started laughing and joked about how sensitive she was through the rest of the meeting. She reported many of the men were her friends, and she absolutely believes they did not mean to invalidate her experience; they were doing it unconsciously.

✳ **Microinsults (often unconscious).** "Behaviors/verbal remarks or comments that are rude or insensitive and stem from the privileged person's views about race or identity."

Example: One young Latinx student I met at a workshop confided in me that White students often tell her she's "lucky to be there," implying she got into MIT on affirmative action. Most of the White students there come from wealthy or academic families who have been giving them support throughout their lives, which landed them at MIT. They were the lucky ones. Despite being born very poor, spending time in foster care, and overcoming racial barriers, this young woman had made it to MIT. Luck did not gain this young woman entry into one of the most selective colleges in the world. A brilliant mind, unusually high levels of grit, and hard work did.

The term *microaggressions* was birthed from macropolitical issues, but often micropersonal microaggressions are used to make us feel unsafe in a space. While primarily used by privileged groups to disempower oppressed groups, microaggressions occur any time one person uses subtle, insidious psychological tactics, whether consciously or unconsciously, in an effort to diminish another person's sense of reality, dignity, or self-worth. They are usually perpetrated by people with more power in order to diminish someone with less. Men do it to women. White people do it to people of color. Wealthy people do it to poor people.

With this expanded definition in mind, I've created a longer list of how to identify microaggressions.

Identifying Microaggressions

SUBTLE INSINUATING

Once Chaz, a man I dated for a short time, said this to me: "You know, I realized the other day that you don't have any hobbies. I had a really hard time getting you a birthday present because of it." I found the comment odd as I go to the gym every day, ride my bike, act, direct, and mentor. I volunteer to help political candidates. I work with at-risk youth. I've also been able to parlay what I love—writing, mentoring, public speaking, and so on—into my job. My career is a combination of many of my interests, and I'm so thankful for that. This man had been trying to get me to participate in his hobbies, even though at the beginning of the relationship I had been clear with him that if we were to date I would not be doing things like swimming in ice cold water in the dead of winter with him. When I stood my ground, Chaz tried to slowly get me to judge my "hobbies," insinuating they weren't really hobbies. I needed a hobby, and I should do his hobbies, which were actual hobbies. Needless to say, we are no longer together.

BACK-HANDED COMPLIMENTS

I'm realizing I learned a lot about microaggressions from Chaz. A microaggression expert, he often said things like "You have such a pretty face, and I usually don't find women who aren't very thin attractive, but I can tell I really love you because I like your body." This microaggression is almost always a dig couched as a compliment. If you can roll in some societal judgments about the person you are talking to, like women and body image, all the better! (Wondering why I stayed with this man at all? See the introduction to part 3. Similar to Brad, he was my walking kryptonite. Sometimes you have to learn a lesson more than once.)

DIMINISHING "JOKES"

One great way to get a dig in without being called on it is to turn the dig into a joke. During Q&A after a workshop I gave, a woman told a story of being in a meeting after having closed a huge deal. She was the only woman at the table. Her boss congratulated her in front of everyone and then said, "Now, Angelica, be sure not to go out and buy a new purse with all that money." Her colleagues laughed. She was flabbergasted and embarrassed.

REALITY BENDING

A client of mine is not only the only woman in her department, but the only woman of color. She worked in a department where everyone wore jeans. While walking into her boss's office, she ran into a senior colleague, who was leaving. He said to her with a smile on his face, "Wow. You must really be making a statement going to talk to him in jeans." She was floored. Everyone wore jeans. Her colleague was wearing jeans that very moment, having just met with their boss! And yet somehow she suddenly felt bad about wearing jeans. In fact, when she told the story, she said, "I mean, my jeans are *nicer* than everyone else's!" That moment had warped her reality to the point where she couldn't see this simple fact: it didn't matter how nice or not nice they were. Everyone else wore them, so she should be able to wear them as well without comments.

PHYSICAL BOUNDARY BREAKING

This of course can escalate to sexual harassment. However, it's important to note that it often starts much more subtly than that. The classic example of this is a White person asking if they can touch a Black woman's hair. White people, please don't do this. Not ever. Don't ask to rub the pretty fabric on a woman's clothing. Don't ask to touch her earring. Don't loom over her à la the Trump versus Clinton debate. Just don't. Respect personal space. And seriously, never, ever ask to touch a Black woman's hair. Ever.

GROUP CLUMPING

Telling someone they are a certain way because they belong to a certain group is a microaggression, even if you think it's nice. "Of course you're smart! You're Asian!" or "I've noticed a lot of my ex-girlfriends don't make sense around the time of their period." Talk about the individual, not the group they belong to.

DESTRUCTIVE COMPARING

This is a tactic used by people who want to undermine another person's experience. So, for example, you say as a woman you don't like it when men at work compliment the way your clothes fit. The man then says, "But I've talked to X, Y, and Z women, and they all liked it." When people speak from their experience, they will often use secondhand experiences of others in your group to undermine yours.

MANIPULATIVE POSITIONING

One of the most damaging microaggressions is the set-up. This happens when someone knows how to push your buttons, pushes them, and then when you react with anger, tells you you're over-reacting. If someone you know does this, run. (If you work with them and can't run, put up massive boundaries.)

VICTIM SITUATING

After the manipulative positioning, if you find yourself apologizing because you responded to a microaggression, you are experiencing victim situating. Here's an example:

> *Microaggressor:* "Hey, I bet you watched basketball last night. I know [insert name of other Black person in the office] did. How was the game?"

> Target (calmly): "You know, I'm wondering why you mentioned me and the only other Black person in the office. I've noticed you often lump us together."

Microaggressor: "Wow. You are so sensitive. I was just trying to make conversation!"

Target (calmly): "OK. I'm sorry."

An aggressor positioning himself as the victim after he has goofed is a powerful microaggression.

Combating Microaggressions

Once you know what microaggressions are, you're ready to learn to combat them.

1. **Name the aggression.** Name the type of microaggression. Is this an insult, invalidation, or assault? If not, does it fall into one of the categories I covered? Once you have decided, name it in your head. "What that person just did is group clumping."

2. **Reality check.** Tell yourself your gut is not lying to you. What happened did indeed happen. Your experience is real.

3. **Decide.** Determine if you think the microaggression rises to the level where you need to call it out. Oppressed groups experience isms every day. We can't possibly call them all out. That's all we would do. Whether to address a microaggression is a deeply personal choice. Everyone must set their own boundaries.

4. **Safety check.** Consider whether it is safe to call it out. Could calling it out put your emotional or physical safety at further risk? Could calling it out hurt your financial situation, meaning it would put your job/promotion/hiring at risk? If you are in a room with no allies, it might not be the time. If you have a strong ally in the room who will back you up, then you might choose to go for it. If you are with a partner trying to kill all traces of sexism in order to better your relationship, then absolutely address it. Don't expose yourself to more microaggressions by calling them out at the wrong time.

5. **Ask.** This lies at the heart of interrupting microaggressions. *The best way to combat microaggressions is to ask a question.* Let's

revisit the jeans example. One response to that might be, "I'm wondering why you're asking me about my jeans when everyone else is also wearing jeans."

6. **Shut up.** After you ask the question, shut up. It's tempting to jump in and make the microaggressor comfortable. Don't. Let the uncomfortable silence linger. (Remember the power of silence. Now's one of those times to wield it!)

7. **Don't apologize.** This is the moment your interruption of the microaggression can be hijacked. This is the cycle I see with my clients:

   a. They call out the microaggression.

   b. Microaggressor says, "Wow, you hurt my feelings."

   c. They say, "Oh, I'm sorry."

   This results in the microaggressor feeling vindicated and having learned nothing. You, on the other hand, feel nuts. If the person you are talking to positions himself as a victim, don't fall for it. Bring it back to the question. "I hear you're feeling bad about this, but what I'm wondering is why you [insert microaggression]."

8. **Redirect.** If they begin to attack you, use the "the issue is, the issue is not" strategy. The jeans example would sound like this: "*The issue is* I'm wondering why you asked about my jeans. *The issue is not* about if I'm overreacting."

9. **Take time out.** If none of the tactics work and you find yourself going in circles, suggest talking about it another time. That will give the person time to reflect on what happened and you time to think of different strategies when you're not in the heat of the moment.

There is no reason another human should ever, ever leave you feeling undermined, angry, confused, and hurt. Learn to see microaggressions, trust what you see, name them, and stop them. This can be tiring. But you can do it. Trust. Name. Stop. Then, until we live in a better world, rinse, repeat.

INTERRUPTIONS

The number one reason I'm unable to leave the bathroom after I give a talk can be summed up in one word: interruptions. Women are pissed off about being interrupted. Talk about claiming space! People literally shutting down your words and ideas by stopping you midsentence with what they deem to be a more important thought? Yeah, that's a great way to make a woman small.

If you already know how to shut down or prevent all interruptions with zero effort, then you are a magical unicorn and I want to know your secret! If you are like 99.99 percent of the rest of us, then welcome to being a woman with a pulse. For non-unicorns, interruptions can feel like weeds. You get one under control right as another pops up out of nowhere. If you have reached the end of your patience with interruptions, fear not. With a little effort you can banish this pesky problem and claim space like a carefree unicorn.

A Brief History of Verbal Interruptions

For centuries women resigned themselves to being interrupted. Interruptions happened at school, home, work, even when we were talking to our doctor about that really embarrassingly placed mole we just found. They happened so much, we often didn't notice. Then, slowly, this issue moved from gender studies departments to boardrooms and bedrooms all over the country. Women went from "I guess I need to shut up because he's talking" to "Wow! I never noticed that dude won't let me finish my sentence!"

First, let's get clear. Statistically it is men who do most of the interrupting. This is not because men are diabolical supervillains intent upon driving women nuts by taking up all the airspace. Men interrupt more because as little boys they were told by their parents and other adults around them to "stop interrupting" far less than little girls. It's worth noting that dads, moms, and adults of all genders in their lives do this. Therefore, boys learn to talk over people and interrupt, and girls learn to politely shut up. Unfortunately, these communication patterns follow us into adulthood. I first read about this in a *Slate* article by Kieran Snyder titled "Boys Learn to Interrupt. Girls Learn to Shut Up."[1] After reading that article, I realized that as a parent I had observed this phenomena over and over again but never noticed it. In hindsight, it was so glaring I couldn't believe I missed it before. Now, I see it whenever I'm with young kids. In every situation where little girls and boys were speaking, girls were disproportionately told to stop interrupting and boys were allowed to interrupt almost without any checking at all. I live in a town that identifies as progressive. The kids in this area were unequally schooled in interruption expectations no differently from kids I interact with when traveling in conservative areas of the country. If we want to attack this at its roots, parents everywhere must be sure we are teaching all of our kids not to interrupt at the same rate.

Handling Interruptions, Gently

Speaking of being a kid, if you were like me as a little kid and always wanted to learn to wield the Force, now's your moment. Remember when Obi-Wan uses the Force and says, "These aren't the droids you're looking for"? I will admit I'm still deeply disappointed I can't move things with my mind, but learning this technique to stop interruptions is a close second.

It's a four-step process, but you can usually stop all interruptions without much fanfare before step 3. My clients consistently report this technique works close to 100 percent of the time.

Some women *do not* want to shy away from drawing attention to the interruption. They want to address it head on, consequences be damned. If you don't just want to stop interruptions but instead wish to address them head on, great! Please skip to the section "Prepare Your Offensive for Their Defense(iveness)" later in this chapter. I'll teach you how.

For those who want to stop the interruptions without drawing attention to them, here's how you use the Force à la Obi-Wan with the Stormtroopers. Please use the following handy cartoon as a guide as you read. Cartooned space claimers, from top to bottom, are Katie (my "sister"), Lynn (illustrator), and Ella (my daughter!).

Channeling the Force

**STEP 1: KEEP TALKING. (YOU'RE NOT A JEDI YET.
NO FORCE HERE.)**

Get a little louder and *keep talking over the interruption.* This should work 100 percent of the time. Sadly, it does not. It works about 50 percent of the time but is worth a shot before summoning the Force.

**STEP 2: THE FINGER WARNING.
(STILL NOT THE FORCE.)**

Put *one finger up* with your palm facing the person who is interrupting you, and with a smile, say one or two words.

Examples:

- "Excuse me."
- "One sec."
- "Sorry."

After saying these words, keep talking. *Never* wait for a response.

Some women bristle at the idea of saying sorry, particularly with a smile, when someone is interrupting them. My answer is twofold.

1. This is the gentle approach. Again, if you prefer going to war, skip to the following section.

2. If you take this approach in front of others, and use the casual platitudes I enumerated, an ally may notice the interruption and shut it down for you.

STEP 3: THE ONE-HANDED WARNING.
(THE FORCE!)

Put *one hand up* with your palm facing the person who is interrupting you, and with a hint of a smile, say a phrase like one of these examples:

- "Hold on a sec."
- "Excuse me. I'm talking."
- "I'd like to finish."

Then keep talking. Never wait for a response.

At this point you have already drawn attention to the interruption twice, both with your words and your body. Now you're drawing even more attention with a bigger gesture, which accomplishes two things:

1. It lets the interrupter know, through verbal and physical cuing, they are pushing their luck.

2. Those around you can't miss what's happening. Often at this point, an ally will step in and say, "Hey, I'd like to hear Eliza finish." I can't lie. I love it when this happens, and by this stage, it happens fairly predictably.

STEP 4: THE TWO-HANDED FORCE.
(CHANNEL PRINCESS LEIA!)

Raise *both hands,* again with your palms facing the interrupter. Then, *without blinking or even a hint of a smile* on your face . . . say the following phrases:

- "Excuse me. I'm talking."

- "I'd like to finish."

- "May I please finish?"

Women are expected to make men comfortable when we communicate. This is a departure from that expectation. It consistently results in the interruptions stopping because

- It scares the crap out of the interrupter.

- Other men often jump in to help, even those who aren't usually sensitive to interruptions.

Prepare Your Offensive for Their Defense(iveness)

There is a point when we've had it. Something awakens in us, and we decide we don't want to use the Force. We want to shut down interruptions directly, and without apology. My daughter and her friends do this, and it's inspiring to watch as they tackle interruptions like the fearless and fierce intersectional feminist space claimers they are. There are, however, ways to do this well and ways that are less effective. Here is the way I have found to be the most powerful.

WHEN YOU TELL A GUY TO STOP INTERRUPTING

Most men have absolutely no idea when and how much they interrupt. On top of this, they usually think it is *other* men who interrupt, and that *those* men are the *real* assholes. This poses a bit of a dilemma when you point out interruptions. Most decent human beings do not want to behave like assholes. Therefore, when you point out behaviors associated with being an asshole, it is predictably human for the other person to have a less than optimal, and very defensive, reaction.

The pushback you will receive comes in three delicious flavors. Be prepared for them.

FLAVOR 1: DENIAL

"I didn't interrupt you. That never happened. Nope. Not *ever!*"

This flavor could also be called Gaslighting 101.

The challenge here is that people will *never* change their minds once they have dug deep into the "that never happened" hole.

Strategy: There's no room for conversation here. Simply say, with channeled anger, "I'm not debating this. I know what I experienced. Don't do it again." Remember my favorite quote from *A Wrinkle in Time*? Stay angry, little Meg! Make unblinking eye contact and play high!

Outcome: This will not work in the short term. They will probably deny it again, and get angry. There is, however, a light at the end of this tunnel. *People who deny reality like to prove they are right.* So, in the future, these interrupters will try *not* to interrupt in order to prove they never interrupted when you called them out on interrupting. Check. Mate.

FLAVOR 2: BLAME SHIFTING

"Well, you interrupted *me* first, so why are you on *me* about interrupting?! *Interrupter!*"

At this point you have a choice. Do you mention that yes, perhaps you have interrupted (if you have), but they have consistently been interrupting far more? Do you point out that you were really just trying to finish your sentence, *a sentence they interrupted*, when you interrupted them?

I recommend doing neither of these, as they won't work. Instead, use a similar strategy to flavor 1, but with a twist.

Strategy: Say "I'm not debating this. I know what I experienced. I am simply asking you not to interrupt *so frequently*."

Outcome: Folks who do this are also stuck in a right-and-wrong paradigm. By saying "frequently," you put the bug in their ear that they are interrupting a lot. As they must be "right" in order to prove they don't interrupt frequently, they will reduce their rate of interruptions in the future to prove you wrong. Again . . . checkmate.

FLAVOR 3: THE CRAZY FEMINIST BITCH DEFENSE[1] (OR "THE CLASSICS")

"Wow. You're being such a bitch!"

> or

"Do you have to be so crazy and high strung about it?"

> or

"What are you? Some kind of *feminist*?!"

This is one of those delightful moments where we are either called a little crazy or a little bitchy or a (gasp!) feminist. What always strikes me in moments like this is the escalation in tone usually is started by the man accusing the woman of escalating. Regardless of how the escalation started, I recommend proceeding with caution.

Strategy: Try a good old-fashioned "The issue is not X; the issue is Y." For example, "The issue *is not* whether I'm [crazy, a feminist, a bitch, and so on]; the issue *is* I'd like you to stop interrupting me."

You could also call out that they are using gender-specific words meant to silence you in response to you telling them to

---

[1] Go to part 3, chapter 8 for a handy refresher on this delightful strategy!

stop silencing you. I fully relate if you want to do this. I often do it myself. Just keep in mind the conversation will immediately hop to yet another conversation: their justification of those words and your educating them about said words, rather than the interruption. That's your call. Pick your battle. If the person uses silencing words a lot to try to make you small, you might want to go for it. If they are world-class interrupters, try to stick with that.

Outcome: There is no predictable outcome when this happens, but be prepared to walk if you need to. People who pull out these diminishing words are often not safe, and unable to engage in thoughtful conversation. That said, I have been proven wrong on many occasions and had fruitful conversations with folks who initially tried to weaponize those words to silence me.

It would be pretty unfair if I didn't talk about the final response you might get. It's not flavor 4, because it's not a form of pushback. But it is importat to mention.

THE (SHOCKING) APOLOGY

"Golly, that just really isn't OK behavior on my part. Thanks for pointing it out. I try so hard not to interrupt, and I'll redouble my efforts in the future. I shall also strive, day in and day out, to be a perfect ally. *Down with the patriarchy!*"

As dear brother Alek said dryly when I read him a draft of this chapter, "That's stretching it."

Joking aside, men like Alek do say this:

"Was I? I had no idea. Sorry about that. You were saying?"

Thanks to a little education from the women in their lives and the changing attitudes of our younger generation, men like Alek seem to be increasing in number exponentially. Thanks, guys—you're amazing!

Strategy: Say "Thanks for listening without getting defensive. I appreciate it!"

Outcome: Saying thanks is always a good idea when people do the right thing. By doing so, you are reinforcing their good behavior, and who can argue with that outcome?

If you want to engage in open combat, despite pushback, I thank you. You are a special breed of superhero; claim space not just for yourself but for all other women! As Wonder Woman says, "If no one else will defend the world, then I must." Thank you for being our real live Wonder Woman!

MANSPLAINING

Dear Gentlemen,

This section is largely for you. Why? Because this problematic communication is solely your fault. Perhaps not *your* fault specifically, but *mansplaining* is most certainly the fault of men. Therefore, it is not our problem to solve. It's yours. But take heart; I wrote this chapter specifically for the men committed to making a difference . . . the superhero allies in our lives. Unless you're reading this because another man gave it to you to stop your unceasing interrupting, that's you! We, the women in your lives, thank you in advance for using the strategies in this book to interrupt any and all mansplaining. Dealing with sexist behavior can be a challenge. We know. We've been there. We thank you in advance for striving to be as smart as Batman, as kind as Captain America, as empathetic as Spider-Man, and as brave as Superman as you embark upon this honorable journey.

—**Warmly, Eliza**

And now, story time!

Let's start with my favorite mansplaining story. Hopefully you will find it as gallows-humor funny as I do. Admittedly it's not the grandest mansplaining story of all time. It does, however, perfectly illustrate why mansplaining is so very hard for women to combat.

Several years ago I was producing a play. Most of our team was composed of men, and we were working on a project for a CEO, Trey, who tended to favor men's voices. This was more than a bit frustrating at times. Indeed, I was about ready to pop on the regular.

Here's what would happen.

1. I would offer an opinion.

2. It would be succinctly discarded or ignored.

3. Jack, a funny, charming, and brilliant man I've known for years, would notice this was happening.

4. Jack would chime in to "help" me by saying, "I think [insert thing I just said, using almost all of my words, to the letter] is a great one because . . ."

5. After Jack spoke, my idea would be heard.

6. The idea would be adopted as an excellent one! (Yay.)

7. And sometimes even credited to Jack. (Double. Yay.)

At first I questioned whether I was losing my mind. The mansplaining was just *so* obvious, yet no one seemed to notice except Jack, and how was it he couldn't tell he was making things worse? Then, after devoting one meeting to carefully watching the communication dynamics, I reassured myself of the following: Mansplaining was, indeed, happening. It was, indeed, majorly undermining me. And it was, indeed, seriously pissing me off.

So, how to handle it? I knew the men in the group saw themselves as enlightened feminists who believed they had figured out how to never, ever participate in sexism. This group is particularly hard to deal with. I decided the best plan of attack was to go to my closest ally, Jack.

"Um, Jack, have you noticed when you endorse my ideas they get traction, even though you have zero background in my field?"

My sweet friend began to positively glow, proud of his efforts to be my ally. "Yeah. It's annoying. You have great ideas! That's why I always make sure to repeat them for you. Because Trey listens to me."

This is one of those moments that reminded me that most people have good intentions, even if the impact of their actions isn't always so great. Thankfully, I'm close with Jack, so I dove right in without worrying too much about pushback.

"Jack, you know I adore you and absolutely know you're trying to help, but when you repeat what I say as if I wasn't clear, you're not really helping. Actually, you're undermining me."

Jack looked shocked, then stricken, then absolutely mortified. He had been born into abject rural poverty in the South and had a thick accent that revealed to many where he grew up and how much money, or lack thereof, his parents had. He was also the first to go to college in his family. When Jack first arrived at Princeton, he felt out of place. In many ways, he was. Jack had grown up in an entirely different world from so many of his fellow students, many of whom came from old money. For this reason he mindfully worked hard to never contribute to others' oppression. He had experienced what it was like to be an outsider. He never wanted to make others on the outside feel they should be silenced or they didn't belong. After I stopped talking, Jack got quiet for a bit and then said, "Well, damn! I'm doing the opposite of what I'm trying to do!"

"I know you're not meaning to," I said, "but you are kinda perpetuating the idea that a woman's voice doesn't have validity unless—"

Jack interrupted me midsentence, no joke! "It's backed up by a man. *I get it.* Silences women's voices! OK. What's your advice? You always have some! Give it to me."

"Well," I said, pondering whether he had noticed he'd just silenced mine, "the best thing to do is to simply say, 'I agree with

Eliza.' If they ask why you agree, just throw the ball to me: 'What she said was clear to me, but Eliza, maybe you could explain it again?' At that point I can jump in and say it myself."

Jack's eyes popped open, then he started laughing his warm, welcoming laugh. "Damn. Well *that's* pretty straightforward!" You'd think the story would be over now . . . but the best is yet to come! Jack then launched into a lengthy monologue/speech/diatribe/lecture about an article he had recently read on mansplaining in *The New York Times*, and how crappy women feel when it happens, and how diminishing it was to women, and so on. My well-meaning, dear friend mansplained me during a conversation about how he was contributing to mansplaining by telling me (thus mansplaining) how I felt about mansplaining . . . and he had no clue he was doing it!

I decided I had bigger fish to fry than the current quagmire of mansplaining, and we wrapped up our conversation. The very next meeting, Jack stepped in like a champ, stopping the mansplaining in its tracks with zero pushback—a very different outcome than if I had tried to address it. Once our project was over, we went out for drinks to celebrate. That's when I brought up his hilarious mansplaining about mansplaining moment. He took it like a champ and we laughed till our stomachs hurt. To this day, I'm still not sure if I should have called him out at the time. Knowing when and how to talk to allies is a fine art you can get better at but never fully master.

Should women be heard when they call out behaviors that are harmful to their careers? Yes. But the research is unequivocal. The dominant group is far more likely to listen without defensiveness to similarly situated members of their group. So, whenever possible I try to pull in allies to interrupt moments of sexism.

And now, readers of all genders, please enjoy these handy guides to different kinds of mansplaining. May they serve as your guide! Thank you to my dear friends who posed for the drawings! Yes, my little brother Alek does bear a striking resemblance to Jerry Garcia.

THE "HIJACK"

A WOMAN'S CONTRIBUTION IS ABOUT TO BE IGNORED!

IN THIS SCENARIO, THE WOMAN, PAIGE, OFFERS A NEW IDEA... PAIGE: "I'm thinking we should kick off our PR campaign in March because of Women's History Month."

MINUTES LATER, THE HORRENDOUS HIJAK! (OH NO!)

MICHAEL THE MANSPLAINER:
Ya know, it occurs to me that we should definitely start PR for this client in March! That's Women's History Month!

SUDDENLY, LISTENERS DEVELOP AMNESIA, CREDITING THE HIJACKER FOR HIS GREAT IDEA! (DANGER!)

IT'S TIME FOR...
FIRST AID FOR MANSPLAINING!

DARRYLE THE ALLY:
Paige suggested a March PR campaign a few minutes ago. Michael just repeated what Paige said. Her idea has become his idea, and all are in favor. We need to examine that.

IF NO ALLY...

PAIGE THE SPACE CLAIMER: Michael just repeated what I said. I'm wondering why my idea is being adopted and credited to him, when he just restated what I said?

THE "'EXPERT' NON-EXPERT"

A WOMAN'S EXPERTISE IS ABOUT TO BE DEVALUED!

IN THIS SCENARIO, THE WOMAN, LESLYN, SHARES HER SUBJECT MATTER EXPERTISE . . .

LESLYN: "My extensive research, and 20 years of experience in advertising, leads me to believe we should use red in our campaign."

WITHOUT HESITATION, THE EGREGIOUS "'EXPERT' NON-EXPERT" OPINION! (UH-OH!)

THE "CLARIFICATION"
A WOMAN'S VOICE IS ABOUT TO BE DIMINISHED!
IN THIS SCENARIO, THE WOMAN, PRACHI, SPEAKS CLEARLY . . .
PRACHI: "The research shows clearly that our target audience is 25- to 35-year-olds."
MERE SECONDS LATER, THE CALAMITOUS "CLARIFICATION"!! (YIKES!)
STEVE THE MANSPLAINER: I think what Prachi meant to say is that research clearly shows that our target audience is between 25 and 35.
VOILA! THE CROWD SUDDENLY GETS IT! (RED ALERT!)
IT'S TIME FOR . . . FIRST AID FOR MANSPLAINING!
TYREE THE ALLY: I understood what she said and I'm in full support of it! Thanks, Prachi!
IF NO ALLY . . .
PRACHI THE SPACE CLAIMER: Actually, that's not what I "meant to say." It's what I said. Thanks for backing up my idea!

Physical violence, bullying, interrupting, mansplaining . . . some are worse than others, but all are not OK. All seek to keep us small by instilling fear in us. We need not be "nice" and accept this. Call it out. Shut it down. Recruit an ally. Never, ever allow yourself to believe for one moment that feeling unsafe in any space is something you need to live with.

And let's teach the little Megs in our lives, the little girls we know and love, it's OK to be angry. Let's teach them how to claim space safely in any space, and that claiming that space is a fundamental human right. Let's teach them to stay loud, stay opinionated, and stay angry.

May they grow up to be unstoppable women who can claim space wherever they go, with anger, and without apology.

PART 5

CLAIM

SPACE

UNITED

Commit to Intersectionality!

Create a better world for us all.

I am not free while any woman is unfree, even when her shackles are very different from my own.

—AUDRE LORDE

Women must be treated fairly. We have the right to claim space equally and without pushback.

Scratch that. Old, young, rich, poor, Black, Brown, Tan, Indigenous, Alaska Native, White, Christian, Jewish, Muslim, Bahá'í, Buddhist, agnostic, atheistic, rural, urban, conservative, progressive, socialist, anarchist, able bodied, people with disabilities, neurotypical, neurodivergent, trans, cis, fluid, genderqueer, agender, bigender, straight, binary, femme, lesbian, gay, bi, pan, and queer women need to be treated fairly.

Do you feel uncomfortable?

Are some of these terms unfamiliar to you?

Do you feel like maybe that's overkill?

If your answer was "yes" to all three, I promise you're not alone. Most people don't like thinking about or talking about what makes us different. Therefore, we don't often learn terms and concepts we really should. Instead, we like to talk about the things we have in common—it's more comfortable. It's easier. That's why we tend to gravitate toward people who look like us, think like us, and have similar experiences.

Here's the problem with focusing only on our sameness. On every corner of the planet where you find humans, you will find women, and while we share so much in common, there are experiences we can never share. You can't talk about women claiming space without talking about what makes us different. Until we understand our differences, we won't understand each other, and as long as we don't understand each other, we are divided. Divided, we are vulnerable. For years when I thought of advocating for women, I didn't realize I was thinking of advocating for women like me, White upper-middle-class women. This, of course, was a flawed perspective. "Woman" does not equal "White woman."

Part of how we have been kept from claiming space is that we align with our race, our religion, our politics, or other things that divide us, rather than our womanhood. If you don't understand

What other women are going through, how can you possibly stand side by side with them in sisterhood? You can't.

* **Divide a group and they cannot claim space effectively.** No woman can rise as high if any of us expend time and energy avoiding, competing with, or fighting each other.

* **A group united is powerful.** Women have vastly different experiences and skills, and this is our strength. Together, we are situated to tackle any challenge.

* **When 51 percent of the human race unites . . .** A group united composed of slightly more than half the population? That group is unstoppable.

The more varied experiences you are exposed to, the more you understand the world. The more you understand the world, the more likely you are to succeed in it both personally and professionally. The chapters in this part are about claiming space for others, something that not only is the right thing to do, but also increases your ability to claim space for yourself by orders of magnitude. If you are new to the idea that "feminism" is not a dirty word, by now I hope you are proudly embracing your inner crazy feminist bitch. I'm now going to add another term to your arsenal of awesome words to wear proudly and without apology: "intersectional feminist." What does that mean? In short it means this: Feminists leave no woman behind, even if a category she falls into is foreign, or even scary, to us. Just as we ask men to do, we learn, we listen, and we believe our sisters. Then we stand by them, unwavering, knowing that we are helping every woman every time we do this.

To use a quote by Flavia Dzodan my daughter has hanging in her dorm room, "My feminism will be intersectional, or it will be bullshit."

How Two Worlds Can Exist in One Place

For years I thought I had a handle on one of the categories that divides us most: race. My schizophrenic mother had taken me from my father, illegally. Eventually, I was found by the police and landed in foster care as my parents battled for custody in court. I was the only White girl in an all African American foster care home. My neighborhood was composed exclusively of Brown and Black people. Although I was treated very well by everyone I met, I did experience being the "other." I had always thought this experience lent me insight into race. It did not. I experienced what it was to be different, and BIPOCs do experience that all the time when they are numerically outnumbered. I did not, however, experience the added difficulty my BIPOC sisters experience: people treating me poorly because of my race. In fact, folks went out of their way to be nice to me. Young children of color in predominantly all White neighborhoods often experience just the opposite.

I started to understand how much I could never understand about race when I was a young mother and two young families moved next door to me. I became dear friends with the moms and fell in love with their children. Kim had two daughters, her younger daughter Mirana, who is Black, and Kieren, who is White. Saskya had two daughters as well, Prachi, who is Brown and of Indian origin, and Meike, who is White.

That's when everything began to shift. I listened as these mothers confided in me about the radically different treatment their universally well-behaved, kind, delightful daughters experienced. I heard the pain in their voices as they told of what their Brown and Black daughters were going through. I realized I had absolutely no idea what it was like to live as a Black or Brown person in this country, not a clue. The more I heard the stories, the more my heart broke. It felt as if I were going through a death. I realized the world I lived in was a parallel universe, one where I could go seven miles over the speed limit without worrying about getting pulled over, walk through a store without being followed, and not worry my child (or I) would be given suboptimal care in the hospital.

I remember the first story that nearly broke my heart in half. Mirana had gone to school to get help from her seventh grade math teacher. Kim told Mirana to make sure to go to the front office and get a pass before going to her teacher. She watched from her car as Mirana walked to the office for a pass. She watched as her beloved daughter walked out of the office without a pass and then diligently walked to the hall monitor. She watched as Mirana waited in line for her turn to go past the hall monitor. Sweet little White child after sweet little White child went in front of sweet Mirana without showing a pass. Then, it was the sweet little Black child's turn. Kim saw Mirana talk briefly to the hall monitor, put her head down, and walk dejectedly away. She watched as Mirana stood alone in the hallway, her big backpack dwarfing her little body, still staring at the floor . . . looking alone and lost.

Kim was in the school like a shot. She walked up to Mirana and asked what had happened. Mirana quietly told her she had asked the front office for a pass. They told her she didn't need one. Mirana had said her mom told her to get one, and they told her to stop being difficult and just go to her teacher—the hall monitor wouldn't give her trouble. Mirana walked up to the hall monitor and despite the fact that many little White girls in front of her had been waived through without a pass, he told Mirana to go get a pass. He didn't believe she could be in accelerated math.

After hearing the story, Kim, a fiercely devoted mom, walked into the front office and called the principal out of his office. "Why didn't anyone give Mirana a pass?" The principal told Kim that Mirana didn't need one. Kim flew out the door and brought the hall monitor into the office, and he admitted he had not let Mirana pass. Kim looked at the room and said evenly, "I think you're going to need to examine the fact that six little White girls went in front of my daughter and none were asked for passes. I also want to put you on notice. When this child asks for a pass, you will give her a pass, because she clearly will need one."

Kim lived to the right of my house. Saskya lived behind me. My love for their daughters, my young "nieces" who would run around the house playing with my kids, was the beginning of my long and painful journey on race. The stories that I heard from their caring moms broke my heart, and these stories happened weekly, sometimes daily. It was death by one thousand cuts for both of their sweet daughters. As they have become young women, the cuts have only gotten deeper. My love for them has forced me never to look away from what our society does to our sisters of color, and to commit to working for change.

I understand why people don't like to think about race and the other "isms" that separate us. It's painful. If you are White, you realize that the world that you live in is not the same world that other people live in. The process of learning about race feels for many very much like a death. The death of your reality.

But delving into power dynamics also feels like a birth, because you see the world so differently, and you will be changed profoundly for the better. Most of us have a fundamental belief that there should be equality and fairness, yet we really don't have any idea how to go about making that happen. Most of us would also like to have a better understanding of the mechanics of how we communicate, would like to know how to predict behavior, and would like to understand why people treat each other as they do. Learning about race is one of the best ways to achieve all of this. The more I understand women whose experiences are different from my own, the more I understand the world. That understanding of the world has helped me in every aspect of my life: my personal life, my professional life, my friendships, and even my romantic life have benefited. The more I understand and advocate for my sisters, the more I can understand and advocate for myself. The space that I claim alongside my sisters who are different from myself augments my own ability to claim space in deep and profound ways.

Today I don't shy away from being uncomfortable. Sometimes I put my foot in my mouth . . . often I put my foot in my mouth. Sometimes I feel embarrassed. Sometimes I feel defensive and angry. But I always learn. I always come out feeling more knowledgeable, stronger, and infinitely more capable of claiming space not just for my sisters but for myself. Few things are more empowering than standing in solidarity with women fighting to claim space.

If you're White, it is my hope this part will serve as a gentle but enlightening guide to what should be a never-ending journey on race and other isms. If you're the target of isms, I thank you for putting up with an entire part of a book you probably already understand through your lived experience. I hope you might find some fun in it, like chapter 18, "How Not to Be a Foke White Person." More importantly, I hope you can use this part as a tool to create conversations with the White people in your life who are open to learning.

When women of all backgrounds learn to listen to, to understand, and to advocate for each other, we will all have an army of women who have our backs.

We must claim space on behalf of women from all backgrounds. Women united, with vastly different experiences and skills, can claim space together in powerfully new and creative ways. Listen to, believe, and advocate for other women. Approach work and life with an open mind and heart. Leave no woman behind.

When we all rise together, we each rise higher.

Why Is This Part So Important?

* **It will help you make *our* world a better place.** If every person isn't able to contribute fully to our society, if some people are unjustly targeted while others have unfair advantages, then we are all diminished.

* **It will help you make *your* world a better place.** Connection with people from all walks of life teaches us to communicate across differences, reflect inward, and stretch out of our comfort zones, and it generally makes us better people.

* **It will help every human claim more space.** The Bahá'í faith says that humanity is like a bird. When one wing is too strong, the bird can't fly right. It seems so simple, but it's true. When one wing is stronger, even that wing isn't flying well. Women united, all women, are a powerful force for change, empowerment, and growth. When all women are more empowered, each and every one of us expands into who we are more authentically and effectively, and we all rise higher.

THE NEED TO BE RIGHT WILL CAUSE YOU TO DO WRONG

Black and white thinking is damaging. The need to feel right can cause you to do wrong. So, the first step to raising each other up is to shift the way we approach right and wrong. Focus on believing others' perspective, and you are on your way to connecting with folks who are different from you.

Good or bad.

Right or wrong.

Moral or immoral.

Seeing the world as black and white causes all kinds of problems. Most importantly, it shuts down your ability to put yourself in other people's shoes and trains you not to believe their reality is real. The foundation of raising up other women is listening to each other, believing each other, and finding solutions together, rather than falling into black and white thinking.

Why are we so tempted to see things in black and white, labeling them as bad or good? We don't just do it in arguments. We do it for all kinds of reasons.

1. **We don't work to really hear someone else's perspective.** It's easier, and more efficient in the short run, to make someone wrong, wrong, *wrong* than to take the time to understand them.

2. **The person we are making "wrong" or "bad" has a quality we really dislike in ourselves.** The old adage that we hate in others what we hate in ourselves really is true. I'm a recovering people pleaser. There is nothing I find more infuriating than, you guessed it, a people pleaser!

3. **In an attempt to make ourselves feel "good," we lower others by making them "wrong."** A great way to know if you're not feeling so good about yourself is to notice whether you spend a lot of time judging other people. I can tell I'm in a crappy place when I suddenly have the urge to start putting others down. I've learned to force myself to try and figure out what's going on with me when this happens. It's a pretty unpleasant process in the short term but tends to make things a lot better in the long run. You can work on yourself while not being a colossal jerk to others, all at the same time!

Feel, Think, Act

So how do you avoid black and white thinking? How do you learn to use the collaborative approach? You have to throw right and wrong out the window and instead approach communication in a wholly different way using this method:

1. Feel.
2. Think.
3. Act.

I realize this sounds incredibly simplistic, and on its face, it is. Implementation, however, can be incredibly hard.

Allow me to explain further . . .

1. **Feel.** Allow yourself to feel the feels. When someone says something to you that makes you want to say, *"You're so very wrong!"* instead try the following.

    Ask yourself, "Self, how do I feel right now?" Identify what you're feeling, then name it. Don't move on to "think" until you are able to get very, very specific. So, for example, "I'm scared and furious this stupid, insensitive person doesn't understand. This all sucks." Then remind yourself there is no such thing as a "wrong" feeling.

2. **Think.** Step out of your feelings for a moment and think. Remind yourself the person you're talking to is also experiencing intense emotions, and they too, are *not* wrong. They just *are*, and their feelings are just as real as yours. Then, armed with your logic, resist removing yourself from the conversation in a huff. Instead, think about how you can express your feelings without making the other person wrong. "I" statements are a safe starting point.

3. **Act.** This is a three-part process.

    a. Say the words you thought in your head out loud.

    b. Shut up.

    c. Listen to the other person's response. Yes, listening is, indeed, an action. Once you hear their response, paraphrase it back to them to be sure you got it, perhaps ending with a "Is that what you're feeling? I want to be sure." Then return to step 1 and do the whole thing over again.

When you first start practicing this, you may feel a bit like Sisyphus. I promise the more you do it, the easier it will get.

Now, here's the vitally important part . . .

The order must be rigid. Feel, think, act. *In that order.* Every time.

This is, by far, the hardest part.

Getting in touch with your feelings can be really hard.

Thinking *before* you take action can be even harder.

And for some, *taking action* can be terrifying, even when you know that's what you need to do.

NEVER SKIP STEPS

If you *skip steps* or do them *out of order*, you will get stuck in a black and white rut.

* **Skipping over the feels.** Attempting to think then act without checking in with your feelings first is like building a house on quicksand. When you don't know what you're feeling, your unconscious often rules the day, and our unconscious can act a lot like an emotionally volatile, impetuous child. Trauma responses are an extreme example of this. People act in ways counter to their own emotional well-being because they aren't in touch with their feelings.

* **Skipping over think.** Learning to *think before you take action* can be frustrating. When emotions are running high, the temptation to skip this step can be huge. If you have ever seen someone yelling in an out-of-control way, that is an excellent example of skipping the "think" stage.

* **Skipping act altogether.** Taking action is often terrifying, even when you know that's what you need to do. Women are champs at skipping this final step. We know what we feel, we have thought out what we should do, but damned if we don't stuff our feelings and thoughts and refrain from acting. This often results in extreme black and white thinking and a complete denial of how the person we are talking to might feel about what we're doing.

Much of the reason we want to kill each other, or at least yell a whole lot, is that we don't take time to process fleeting, seemingly mundane, moments. Our conscious wants to smooth things over, to forget. Unfortunately, our unconscious always remembers, and in the long run, that's when things go off the rails.

Attending to every moment with genuine care is hard, but the payoff is gigantic. And practice really does make perfect. I have committed to doing this more and more, and I can attest that it gets easier and easier the more you do it.

All of your relationships will move to a higher level if you let go of right and wrong. You will no longer draw lines in the sand, decimating others in a painful battle to win at all costs. You will learn to draw a protective circle around you and your potential "adversary." You will become allies, collaborators on a group project with a common, mutually beneficial goal.

Feel. Think. Act. Repeat. Every time.

Healthy human interaction can't happen when there are winners or losers, good guys and bad guys. Someone will always walk away resentful and angry. You can only claim space together when you let go of the battle and approach things as if you are on the same side.

THERE IS A WORLD WHITE PEOPLE CAN NEVER FULLY SEE

The moment you let go of black and white thinking is the moment you can open your heart to listening to the experiences of others. That's when you're ready to start taking in the following truth: White folks can walk on the same streets as folks of color. We often go to the same schools, drive the same cars, and apply for the same jobs as BIPOCs. We even marry and raise children whose skin is different from ours. Yet despite the fact that we inhabit the same spaces, we live in different worlds. Once Whites begin to let this in, our hearts compel us to change things, so that we all rise together. All of us.

Dr. Nunn equates the process White people go through when discovering race to little kids discovering letters. When kids are little, they don't know the letters they are looking at are, indeed, letters. They just see squiggles. When they figure out they are seeing letters, they can't believe it! Those things are letters, and they had always seen them but didn't know it?! When she teaches students about race, she has the same experience. The students start seeing isms everywhere and can't believe they were so blind before. As you get better at understanding race dynamics, you slowly stop seeing only letters and begin to realize they make words, with clear messages on them. It's important to remember that BIPOCs have been reading full paragraphs from the moment they realized they would be treated differently from White people. Imagine their frustration when most of their friends can't even see the letters!

I went through this process of discovering letters myself. Some people call this being woke, but as I will explain later in this part, I think that word is dangerous because it implies there is an "I'm done" on race, and you are never done.

Going back to Dr. Nunn's analogy of discovering letters, I have come to the point where I'm fairly certain I see the letters most of the time. Unfortunately, as a White woman, I constantly remind myself that there are words spelled out clearly, right in front of me, that I have a hard time seeing because of my Whiteness.

This story is one of the harder stories for me to share, as I missed some major words. But it is an experience that I carry with me, a failure, that helps me to always know that I might not know. And that's a huge part of understanding.

A few years ago I was hired to go to a university to give a few talks and run two workshops with a group of grad students. The first day I would be working with them on public speaking in communication, the second day on interview coaching.

I made it very clear to the organizers that people had to do the first workshop in order to attend the second, as they build on each other.

The first day was a lot of fun. The young people were engaged and interested. I had a blast! The next day when I walked in, someone new was there. She was a Black woman named Trina.

I was immediately frustrated. I had explicitly said people had to participate in both days. I was surprised and annoyed that she would come having blown off the first day.

When we went around the table saying names again, the young woman introduced herself as Trina.

"Nice to meet you! You weren't here yesterday," I said, trying to sound neutral, but a bit annoyed.

"No," Trina said, folding her arms and looking defensive and angry, "I wasn't."

I couldn't believe she was giving me attitude! She had blown off the first day!

I gave Trina about an equal amount of time as everyone else, and she was an incredibly quick learner. If I had spent a couple more minutes with her, I probably could've caught her up. But I didn't. In fact, I was a little less invested in her. Why should I go out of my way? She hadn't.

June, the grad student who was my escort around campus, was a dear friend of Trina's. After the workshop, Trina joined us on the way back to the hotel. We had a nice conversation, and Trina said something about how she thought it went well "all things considered." This bothered me even more.

After we parted ways, June shared something with me. Trina had tried to get into the workshop, but she had been blocked out by the limit of fifteen people. The woman who had brought me to this university had decided to give the last spot to a young White woman who was her mentee, instead of Trina. This White woman was far less senior than Trina and, by rights, should never have been let in before her.

After the first session, several friends went to Trina, knowing she had been blocked out. They had had an incredible time at the first session and told her to push to try to get into the second day. Trina battled with the administration for half a day. Eventually, she got in.

"This happens to Trina all the time," June said. "I get in, she's shut out, and a White person with fewer credentials gets 'the thing'—whatever the thing is *that* time."

I was absolutely horrified. Not only had I been angry at Trina, but I hadn't given her the attention I should have after she had worked so hard to get into the second day. Here I was, teaching White people about institutionalized racism, and yet it didn't occur to me that the one Black person who came on the second day might've been facing an institutional barrier. I told June to please offer my heartfelt apologies, that I had been blinded by my Whiteness, and that if she wanted to talk to me, I was open to it. I also told her I would talk to the point person at the university who brought me there. Trina didn't take me up on my offer. One thing I had learned was that when White people mess up around issues of race, we often go to the BIPOC, apologize, tell them how horrible we feel, and wait for them to make us feel better about our racism. It's unfair, as we make the mistake and then expect the person we hurt to take care of our feelings. I never pushed June when Trina said she didn't want to talk. Why should she trust me after how I had behaved? Why shouldn't she think I would not act in her best interest or spend the conversation asking her to forgive me and take care of me? I would have to live with what I had done, which is a lot less than Trina lives with every day.

We must be mindful that the issues some of us face are so systemic that money, power, and access doesn't save us from the power of institutionalized barriers. You can do everything right and you will still be blocked from opportunities by well-meaning White people in power, people like me, who care so much about these issues. Even people who care so much can do significant damage, diminishing others when we are trying to do just the opposite.

White Fragility Is a Barrier to Learning, Hearing, Growing, and Rising

White fragility is the idea that White people have a very hard time talking about race. We have a "fragile" emotional life around the subject. This can lead to us having very negative reactions when confronted with issues of race.

What would you think of a mother who told her daughter the following? "Honey, go to a bar and don't think twice about going home with a random man. Don't put your hand over your drink for fear of being drugged. You're probably safe because most men are not rapists and most men don't drug people. The odds are excellent you'll be OK. Oh, and when you walk home, take the dark alleys. Again, math! The statistics are on your side! Most violence against women does not come from random men jumping out of dark allies."

I'm guessing that sounds downright insane to you.

Most of us have no trouble telling our underage daughters to be careful walking alone at night. Statically, however, our fear is ungrounded. Only 7 percent of underage young women experience sexual abuse at the hands of someone they don't know, while 59 percent are acquaintances and 34 percent are family members. Most nonsexual violence is also not perpetrated by strangers. As for adult women, they are attacked and raped less by random men than men who already know them. The probability of a random man raping our adult daughters is less than one out of five.[1] Yet we warn our daughters to fear strangers. I would argue this is reasonable, as the stakes are incredibly high. (Although we should warn them more about the more common dangers, such as rape on college campuses by men they already know, but I digress.)

Now let's extend this logic to race and see what happens. Women of color live with racially specific aggressions from White folks every day. These range from "subtle" microaggressions at work to death at the hands of the police, even when unarmed.[2] Unarmed Black folks who offer "minimal-to-no threat to police" are three times as likely to be killed by them as their White counterparts.[3]

White people as a group pose a danger to BIPOCs, both emotionally and physically, all day, every day. So why is it we are OK with lumping men together for low-probability behaviors, but lumping Whites together feels grossly unfair to many of us? (For example, "Not all White people are bad! I was totally prejudged, and that's why she misinterpreted what I meant and thought I was being racist! How racist!")

To return to White fragility, here are overarching themes to keep in mind.

1. **Good people are not racist.** Many White folks think of racists as bad people. Therefore, we believe if we do racist things, then we must be bad. One of the best ways to combat racism is to become at peace with the fact that we live in a racist society and therefore are going to be racist, whether we like it or not. So the first step to working on race is to give up the idea of not being racist. Instead, start working to identify your own internalized racism so you can stop its impact.

2. **Secondly, individualism.** BIPOCs are often viewed by Whites as responsible for the actions of their group. Whites view themselves as bearing no collective responsibility for the behavior of other Whites. This is because White folks identify Black, Brown, and Tan people as members of a race. Yet White people are, well, just people . . . colorless.

There is a reason I capitalize White in this book, and why many BIPOC scholars have done so for years. I am recognizing that just like every other group, White folks are a group. By understanding this, we are able to let in this fact: similar to any other group on the planet, we are influenced by members of our group and impacted by how society treats our group.

White women, we must not let our fragility guide us. It is normal for Black folks to have a healthy distrust of White people. We need to accept that our group has done, and does, some pretty horrific things to BIPOCs. It is normal to be lumped in with that group. We are that group.

Also, remember this:

Most Black people cannot talk frankly about race with their White friends. Our fragility makes it too charged and not worth it. If a Black person you know confronts you about your racism, this is often a good sign. It probably means you have earned their trust. They have hope you will see their perspective and hold their truth. Treat that trust the way we all hope a man would treat ours: with an open mind, and with care.

We live in an unfair world. Black and Brown folks know this, as they live it every day. Many White folks want to believe that America is a country with equal opportunity for all. Most of us want the world to be fair, not just for ourselves, but for everyone. Life can be a struggle. It can be very hard when you're struggling to realize that while your struggle is real, others are facing greater barriers.

If you have questions about the inequities so many of our sisters are facing, I hope you'll take a moment to check out the following hard numbers.

Skim the stats on leadership compiled in an article by the Center for American Progress titled "The Women's Leadership Gap" (quoted directly, emphasis added).[4] Women make up 50.8 percent of the population in the United States. Yet look at these numbers. Not one is over 50 percent.

BUSINESS

* "Women of color are *only 4.7 percent* of executive- or senior-level officials and managers in S&P 500 companies."

* "[Women] hold just *19 percent* of S&P 1500 board seats."

* "Women accounted for just 18 percent of all the directors, executive producers, producers, writers, cinematographers, and editors who worked on the top-grossing 250 domestic films of 2017."

LEGAL AND MEDICAL PROFESSIONS

* "In the legal profession, they are 45 percent of associates but only 22.7 percent of partners and 19 percent of equity partners."

✳ "In medicine, they represent 40 percent of all physicians and surgeons but only *16 percent* of permanent medical school deans."

GOVERNMENT

✳ "As of August 2018, [women are] only *23 percent* of the mayors of the 100 largest American cities."

From January 2019

✳ "Women will represent only *24 percent* of members of Congress: 24 percent of the House and *23 percent* of the Senate."

✳ "They will hold *28 percent* of seats in state legislatures."

✳ "They will represent only *18 percent* of governors."

✳ "Women of color represent less than *9 percent* of members of Congress."

White mothers worry their White daughters won't get equal pay for equal work. Mothers who have Brown and Black daughters know that inequity will be even worse for their daughters.

Women of color have a greater wage gap (2020 Census data):[5]

✳ *Black women* working full-time earned *63 cents for every dollar* White men earned.

✳ *Hispanic or Latinx* women working full-time earned only *55 cents for every dollar* White men earned.

✳ *Native American or Alaska Native women* working full-time earned only *69 cents for every dollar* White men earned.

It is worth noting that statistically *Asian women* who work full-time earned *87 cents to the dollar*, while *White women earned 79 cents to the dollar*. Asian women face many forms of racism, but their income is less impacted than their White, Brown, and Black sisters.

White mothers of White daughters worry their daughters will not be granted equal pay or, worse, will be sexually harassed or raped. These worries can keep them up at night.

Mothers of Black boys and men, no matter what their income, worry their sons will live in poverty. They worry their sons will land in jail. They worry their children will leave the house and not come home, dead from gun violence or police brutality.

I can imagine these worries make it hard to wake up in the morning and face another day.

Here are a few hard facts from a *New York Times* article titled "Extensive Data Shows Punishing Reach of Racism for Black Boys" (emphasis added):[6]

* "Even when children grow up next to each other with parents who earn similar incomes, *Black boys fare worse than White boys in 99 percent of America.*"

* "Black men raised in the top 1 percent—by millionaires—were *as likely to be incarcerated* as White men raised in households earning about $36,000."

* "*Black men consistently earn less than White men,* regardless of whether they're raised poor or rich."

* "For poor children, the pattern is reversed. Most poor Black boys will remain poor as adults. *White boys raised in poor families fare far better.*"

What Those Facts Mean for White Women

There are only two ways to look at all of these statistics.

1. Black and Brown people are less intelligent and motivated and are poorly suited for good jobs and leadership positions. In addition, Black and Brown people are naturally more violent, which is why they land in jail and die at the hands of the police more.

2. Society is doing something that disadvantages entire groups of people.

If you think number 1 is likely, you're reading the wrong book . . . and I have some highly effective, expensive snake oil to sell you.

If you chose number 2, let's play a game I learned while studying for my LSATs: the consider-this-logic game.

If you think number 2 is likely . . .

Then you believe the playing field is uneven.

If you believe the playing field is uneven . . .

Then you find the suffering of your fellow American unacceptable.

If you find the suffering of your fellow American unacceptable . . .

Then you must do your part to change things.

Therefore, if number 2 is likely, you must do your part to change things.

17

UNDERSTAND WHAT YOU WERE GIVEN

A few years ago, my daughter was getting ready to apply for college. I was biking down my block and saw my neighbor Clifford sitting on his front porch. I walked up to Clifford and struck up a conversation. I knew that he had worked in admissions at Cornell, the Ivy League university right around the corner from our homes. I wanted advice about my daughter.

Clifford graciously sat down with me on his porch, and we talked for about forty-five minutes. When my daughter came home from school, I passed on the information. Her answer was, "Oh mom! I know his house cleaner's daughter, Marie. She's also applying. I don't think her mom knows that Clifford knows so much about this. Maybe he could talk to her?"

I encouraged my daughter to tell her classmate to have her mother talk to Clifford.

A few days later, I found out what had happened.

Marie's mom explained to Clifford that no one in their family had gone to college and she was a bit lost with the complexities of the process. Could he please give her some advice? Her daughter was a great student, but she didn't know how to support her. Clifford's answer was this: "Of course. I'm happy to help! Just tell her to work really hard."

That's it.

"Just tell her to work really hard."

I, by virtue of being within my neighbor's range of comfort, received his help. I'm a White, educated woman, and he felt comfortable with me.

Others spend a lifetime getting just a sentence . . . "Tell her to work really hard."

The experiences we have make things harder or easier for us. Many of us were fortunate enough to benefit from more opportunities than we realize we did in ways we don't even think about. If we come from a certain privilege, we learn from a young age how to be received well by certain populations, and we learn that we will be received well by those populations. This emboldens us to reach out and gain more information, to network more. My daughter has at least a dozen teachers she has forged relationships with. According to my daughter, Marie doesn't have one, not one. When it came time to get recommendations for college, Marie had to ask teachers who she barely knew. In the end, Marie got into a college well below what her grades and SATs reflected.

It was just the opposite for my daughter. She had spent a lot of time on my metaphorical porch. She was not intimidated by White teachers and in fact was close with many of them. She had also been taught how to talk to people in power through example and direct instruction on my porch. On top of this, I had introduced her to a judge, who had become her mentor. I encouraged Ella to get a recommendation from him and helped her figure out how to ask him. Ella's recommendations were exceptional.

Now, to be fair, as her mama I am the first to say that my daughter is exceptional. But so is Marie. The two things that set them apart are the bricks they carry (race and first gen for Marie) and their time on the metaphorical porch. Marie didn't get hours and hours on my metaphorical porch, teaching her how to communicate with powerful adults through example and direct instruction. She was taught other things on her porch, some of which probably made her the exceptional young woman that she is. But she did not get the skills to navigate power.

Knowing there is a world you can never understand is the first step to every journey on race. Understanding your privilege by examining your metaphorical porch—knowing how much time you got on it and the nature of it—is the second.

The Privilege of Sharing Your Feelings, and When to Shut Up

Sharing your feelings and opinions freely is a privilege. There are many times we should do and say the opposite of what we want to. Identifying those times is critical to building your intersectional justice league. Shutting up is sometimes the best option, even when you're having all kinds of feelings about your feelings.

Recently my friend Polly injured her shoulder and was pretty much incapacitated for two weeks. Her husband, Tyler, stayed home to take care of her during the first three critical days after her surgery. I can attest that the first few days after shoulder surgery are excruciatingly painful. For me, it was a close second to natural childbirth . . . maybe even a tie. It hurts about as much, there are no breaks in between contractions, and you don't get an adorable baby at the end. Needless to say, my friend was in a ton of pain.

Taking care of someone with a shoulder injury is a full-time job. During the first day, Polly's husband was supportive—bringing her food, setting up her medication and icing schedule, and generally doing the things you would hope your partner would do when you're laid flat. Then, on day three, I got a call from Polly. She was in tears. Tyler had started to drop small comments about what a burden it was for him to take care of her. He was falling behind at work. Doing housework solo was overwhelming. The lawn was looking bad. Soon Polly had to deal not only with the pain she was feeling, but also with her feelings of guilt. When she eventually told Tyler that his comments weren't helping the unpleasantness of her situation, the response she got was, "I'm sorry, but I'm just being honest."

Don't be a Tyler. There are times you don't need to share your feelings.

I've found that the extent to which someone can say whatever the hell they want, wherever the hell they want, however the hell they want, is directly related to how much power and privilege that person has. If you want to share your thoughts and feelings with impunity and without consequences, you'd better be pretty damn powerful.

Here's another example. Two friends are sitting together. One is African American and one is White. The White friend is looking at her friend's hair, marveling at how beautiful it is, and suddenly feels the urge to touch it. "Your hair is so beautiful," she says. "Can I touch it?" Her friend gently explains that this is something African American women deal with all the time and calmly says no, she'd really rather not have her hair touched.

Who said what they felt in that situation? Who suppressed their feelings and did not say what they were feeling? As you might have guessed, the White woman expressed her feelings. She wanted to touch her friend's hair. She verbalized what she wanted. Those were her feelings, after all!

Her friend, however, did not express her feelings. Every Black woman I've talked to has reported they are profoundly bothered (read "pissed") when White people ask over and over again to touch their hair. If the Black woman was totally honest, she would have said, "Are you kidding?!" followed by a short lesson on the historic objectification of Black women, followed by, "You know, I really, really hate it that you, someone who claims to care about race, asked such an insensitive question! White people— *argh!*" I don't know if this is exactly what would have been said if she were revealing her true feelings, as I am not this imaginary

Black woman. I do know, however, that the likelihood she would say anything near this level of honesty about her feelings is slim to none.

Black women rarely reveal a great deal of anger when talking to White people, even if it's completely justified. This is especially true at work. Why? The damaging and false stereotype of the angry Black woman results in even the slightest sign of irritation being interpreted as angry and aggressive. This is why Black women have to constantly monitor how they express displeasure to White people. Despite the regular drip, drip, drip of racism and sexism, they must keep their cool, day in and day out. If they said and did whatever they were feeling, whenever they felt it, they could compromise their jobs and maybe even their safety.

When should you speak your mind, and when should you shut up? My handy guide will help you answer this important question . . .

To Shut Up or Not to Shut Up

Avoiding rocking your privilege by oversharing feelings about your feelings when . . .

* **You have power over the person you are talking to.** If you're talking to someone with less power and privilege, unless you're incredibly close, they can't talk to you the way you can talk to them. Recently an African American client of mine was sitting down for a meeting on her first day at a new job. Her boss, who was not involved in hiring her, started the meeting by saying, "Michelle, we all feel happy to have you aboard, and I know how lucky you must feel to be here." This is something people of color hear all the time. White people "earned their spot" but somehow people of color are "lucky to be there." My client was the only person of color in the room, so she smiled, showing no signs of her understandable frustration, embarrassment, and anger. "I wanted to say something," she told me, "but I didn't feel safe." If you're in charge, think

very carefully about the messages you send with your words. Ask yourself if the person you're talking to can respond to what you're saying with anger. Ask yourself, If they had an angry response to your words, could you use social capital to shut them down? If you could, keep your thoughts to yourself.

✳ **The person you are talking to is emotionally or physically vulnerable.** Really being there for someone means helping and supporting without making them feel bad that you're helping and supporting. If you've offered to support someone, don't talk about how hard it is. Go home and have a glass of wine, meditate, or go for a run, but don't share your feelings.

✳ **You are confronted about poor behavior specific to your privilege.** All of us want to feel like we're good people. For most of us, it's incredibly painful to think we did something racist or sexist to someone we care about. If someone musters the courage to share their feelings about an interaction you had, the temptation is to get defensive or overapologize. Remember my story about Trina? *People don't usually want to hear the reason why you did what you did or take care of you because you feel so bad that you screwed up.* They simply want to hear you say "I'm sorry. I acknowledge I did X, Y, or Z, and it angered/hurt/ embarrassed you. I'll work hard to do better in the future." Skip any explanations or oversharing about how bad you feel. Never create a situation where the person who was wronged ends up apologizing to you or taking care of you. (I am quite guilty of overapologizing—it's a constant struggle not to!)

Years ago, I was sitting at my dinner table having a lively conversation with friends. A very thoughtful friend of mine who is White and male was talking about "political correctness." He couldn't understand why he had to use certain politically correct words. "You know, I don't understand why certain words are just off-limits or I have to say things a certain way," he said. "It's crazy! I don't want to be constantly thinking about what I say all the time."

Kim, one of the fiercest allies I have ever known, looked at him, unblinking. Then she gestured to the White women and people of color at the table. "Matthew," she said kindly but firmly, "all of us spend our days navigating around White men in power. We are constantly biting our tongues, thinking carefully about every word that comes out of our mouths. We don't want to be considered 'difficult.' So we constantly handle people all day long—sometimes we don't even know we're doing it, we've been so well trained. But whether we know or not, it's exhausting. You're complaining about having to be careful about a couple dozen words. I think maybe you should examine that."

Now that's how you claim space like a damn boss.

And she was right. We all should.

Developing Perspective

So if we know things have to change, and we have the language, how do we do this?

The first step is the more benign work at the beginning of the chapter. Getting out of black and white thinking and knowing when to shut up. Just keep in mind that White women tend to fall into this kind of thinking when we feel defensive about race. Think back to the previous chapters in this part. Did you ever find yourself uttering phrases like "That's wrong!" or "She doesn't understand that I'm not racist! Not even a little bit!" or "Let me explain why I said that! It's not what you think!" After understanding the problem on a larger scale, the next steps to intersectionality are checking our privilege, understanding our fragility, and developing a feeling that we must be a part of creating change for our sisters facing challenging barriers.

Let's start with privilege. The first step is understanding the burdens and advantages we carry, or don't, as we journey through life. In other words, what's your privilege and what privileges do you lack?

When I talk to people about privilege and advantages, they often get defensive. Indeed, the more power and privilege they have, the more defensive they get. "Look, I worked really hard to get where I am. Are you saying it was *easy* for me?"

No, I'm not. I'm just saying you have to look in your backpack. This concept was inspired by Peggy McIntosh, who wrote the essay "White Privilege: Unpacking the Invisible Knapsack."

Imagine this:

When every one of us is born, we are issued a backpack.

If you're Black or Brown, open up your backpack and put in it a brick with the word "race" etched on the front.

If you're a woman, open up your backpack and put in it a brick with the word "gender" etched on the front.

If you're less attractive, open up your backpack and put in it a brick with the word "unattractive" etched on the front. Why this category? Because "the least attractive [made] 15% less than attractive people in the same position per year."[1]

If you're the first in your family to go to college, open up your backpack and put in it a brick with the words "first gen" etched on the front.

Now imagine that you're a good-looking White man. You're the first in your family to go to college, and you come from a poor family. You're walking up the hill, weighed down with the two bricks "poverty" and "first gen." Your backpack is heavy. This hill is steep. You're sweating. And then someone comes by you on a damn scooter! He's a young White man—he looks very much like you—except he was born wealthy and has had every advantage. His family's power, vast network, and wealth and all the opportunities he's been offered are pushing him up that hill. He doesn't even acknowledge you're there as he blows by you. You're dead tired—it seems so unfair that it's hard to keep walking. Then you hear a group of people behind you yell, "Hey, look at that guy up there. That's not fair!" You know they must be talking about that guy who blew past you—and if they weren't, you have zero energy to turn around. You need to look ahead, nose to the grindstone. "If you're tired, that's your problem!" you yell. You keep walking. You're just so pissed that some people have it so easy!

Eventually, through hard work and perseverance, you're able to remove your poverty brick. You don't notice the people behind you. A few of them, through hard work and perseverance, were able remove their poverty bricks as well. But they are still falling behind.

Why?

They were carrying more bricks from the start, bricks that say "race" or "woman" or "trans" or "unattractive" or "Muslim" or so many other bricks that they will carry throughout their lives. They never get to put them down. To these folks, you look a hell of a lot like that guy on the scooter. And relative to them, you are that guy.

Microaggressions, Redux

Remember when we talked about microaggressions earlier? Remember all the different ways that men could invalidate the experience of women?

Unfortunately, White women often do this very thing to people of color. As I mentioned, the problem with talking about racism is that most people think of racists as people wearing white hoods and pointy hats burning crosses. Nope. Those people are absolutely horrible—they are easy to spot, and you don't question whether they are racist. It's well-meaning people who have a really hard time admitting to themselves that they are racist who can do a huge amount of damage. Their racism flies under the radar in the form of microaggressions.

There is no way you can raise someone up if you're diminishing them. I urge you to go back to chapter 12 for a refresher on microaggressions. If you are a White woman, think about how you felt when reading about them. Now think about how every last one of them is perpetuated by White people against BIPOCs.

Three Forms of Microaggressions

Now that we are diving into race, it's time to revisit microaggressions with a different lens. White women deal with them, but their BIPOC sisters have to navigate the double whammy of both sexism and racism.

As a reminder, these are the three forms of microaggressions according to the 2007 *American Psychologist* article titled "Racial Microaggressions in Everyday Life":

* **Microassault (often conscious).** These are "explicit violent verbal or nonverbal attacks meant to hurt the intended victim through name-calling, avoidant behavior or purposeful discriminatory actions."

  Example: I spoke about the Cornell students in the original example in chapter 12, but it can be far more subtle than that. If you have ever "jokingly" told an Asian woman you were envious of how smart she was because, you know, Asians are good at math, that's a microassault.

* **Microinvalidation (often unconscious).** "Verbal comments or behaviors that negate, or nullify [someone's] psychological thoughts, feelings or experiences." (In other words, what's happening to you isn't really happening. It's in your head.)

  Example: If a person of color has ever shared her experience with you, and you have told her she was mistaken, that what you said had nothing to do with race, or that she was "making it about race" when that's not what you meant, you have perpetuated a microinvalidation.

* **Microinsult (often unconscious).** "Behaviors/verbal remarks or comments that are rude or insensitive and stem from the privileged person's views about race or identity."

  Example: If you have asked to touch a Black woman's hair, even if you never reached for her hair, you have taken part in a microinsult.

It's very important that when someone tells you you did something racist, you say the following to yourself:

1. I will control my fragility.

2. I will let go of right and wrong and believe them.

3. I will understand that even if I don't feel racist, that doesn't mean the impact of my actions, which are an outgrowth of a lifetime of training, wasn't racist.

4. I will simply say, "Thanks for telling me. I'm sorry. I'll try to do it differently next time."

HOW NOT TO BE A FOKE WHITE PERSON

President Barack Obama once said, "This idea of purity and you're never compromised and you're always politically 'woke' and all that stuff . . . You should get over that quickly."[1]

Woke . . . here's how *Merriam-Webster* defines it:[2]

woke \ ' wōk \

woker; wokest

chiefly US slang

: aware of and actively attentive to important facts and issues (especially issues of racial and social justice)

When working on this section, I asked my Brown and Black clients and friends all kinds of questions. One question on the lighter side was, "What's the thing White people do that you find most annoying?"

I got a lot of answers. Here's a sampling of the runners up.

I GET ANNOYED WHEN WHITE PEOPLE ...

"Touch my hair without asking."

"Touch my baby/toddler without asking."

"Explain to me that it's really hard to be Black."

"Ask me questions as if I represent all Black people."

"Cross the street or move their purse when I walk by."

"Question why I won't drive one mile over the speed limit."

"Inform me that I would love *Hamilton*, knowing I hate musicals."

"Say my son is 'like a little monkey' when I'm carry him on my back."

While all of those came up repeatedly, here's a paraphrase of the conversation I had most frequently:

> *Me: "So, what's the one thing White people do that annoys you the most? Not the worst thing ... the most annoying thing."*
>
> *Black or Brown person [chuckling]: "Wow. That's a hard one."*
>
> *Me: "For the purposes of my book, picking only one would be most helpful."*
>
> *Black or Brown person [chuckling]: "Well, I'd have to go with White people who say they're really 'woke.' You can't talk to them when they're acting kinda racist because they think they're 'woke' and 100 percent not racist ... Their heart is in the right place but ... yeah."*

A student of mine, Matt Stupak, made up a word for these well-meaning but confused folks ... *foke*. Matt smushed "faux," which means not real, genuine, or sincere, and "woke" together to come up with this delicious word.

Being foke is a great way to repel people of color from connecting with you.

The rest of this chapter will help you avoid being an annoying foke person. As someone who still struggles at times with being

HOW NOT TO BE A FOKE WHITE PERSON

foke, I had fun writing this, but it was a little humbling. Read on to avoid the sometimes funny, sometimes painful, and always embarrassing pitfalls I have fallen into in the past.

Are You Foke?

Take this fun quiz to find out!

1. **Do your politics exonerate you from all racism?** Do you think being progressive means you're never racist and absolves you from examining your internalized "isms"? If you do, give yourself one point!

2. **Do you like bumper stickers?** Do you talk a lot about how we are "all one people" or perhaps have a bumper sticker on your car that says, "I see no color, because love sees no color"? Do you talk ad nauseum about racial harmony? If the answer is yes, that's one point!

3. **Is Trump the *entire* problem?** Are you very vocal about how much you "hate Trump voters" because they are "all so racist!"? Do you feel you can make a positive impact by yelling at every person you see with a MAGA hat? Most importantly, does attacking others for their racism make you feel all warm and fuzzy inside because it reminds you of how very not racist you are? If so, another point!

4. **Do you talk about *Get Out*? A lot?** Do you tell everyone who will listen about how you watched *Get Out* and totally get race, and by the way, you watched it with your really, really good friend, and by the way, did you mention this friend is Black? He is. He's Black. Five points for this one.

5. **Do you say you're "woke" . . . a hell of a lot?** Do you say this primarily in public? One point! (Give yourself a bonus point if you say this whenever you meet Black and Brown people.)

6. **Are you are a White person who is alive?** Do you feel uncomfortable talking about race? Do you feel odd when you walk

in the room and are the only White person? Do you wish this subject could just be avoided entirely so we could all just get along? Do you sometimes feel like you upset Black and Brown people and you have no idea why? One point.

SCORE THE QUIZ

Ten points: Very foke

My friend, you should probably examine your approach to navigating your Whiteness. I suggest reading anything by Angela Davis, bell hooks, or Robin DiAngelo . . . or at least watching Ava DuVernay's Netflix documentary *13th*.

Two to nine points: Kinda foke

You, like most White folk, struggle to navigate race in this country. You are well meaning, your heart is in the right place, and you're pretty unaware of how much you have to learn about the subject.

One point: Not foke, but not woke

I'm guessing this one point came from question 6. You, like all of us, struggle with internalized racism. You, like all of us, wish this wasn't the case. Read on to understand why if you're White, you can never be woke. But you can do better, learn, and grow.

UNDERSTANDING WHY EVERY WHITE PERSON WILL GET ONE POINT ON THAT QUIZ

With the notable exception of those wearing pointy white hoods, most of us want to believe we are enlightened, thoughtful, and consistently kind to folks different from us. We want to believe only people wearing long white hoods are racist with a capital R.

If only this were true . . .

I wrote that quiz primarily to lighten the mood, but also to illustrate the point that we all struggle with internalized racism.

Understanding Racism, with a Little Help from Sexism

If you're a White woman, a great way to understand race is to think about your experience with men. Men live and breathe sexism every day. We all do, but men, especially White men, usually have the power so their sexism is more damaging. Men can't ever fully stop being sexist, as they will never walk in our shoes. That said, some men seem to do markedly better than others.

THE "I'M A LITTLE SEXIST" GUY

Some men in our lives acknowledge they unintentionally do sexist things, even when they have the best of intentions. These men genuinely listen to women, learn from us, and believe our experiences. (Men of color, who have their own painful experiences with oppression, are more likely to fall into this category. They, too, are often not believed, so they can empathize better outside of their own experience.)

These men exhibit *fewer* sexist behaviors.

THE "I'M NOT SEXIST, NOT EVEN A LITTLE" GUY

Other men think they are never, ever, *ever* sexist. When you try to talk to them about your experiences with sexism, whether or not it's related to them, they won't listen.

These men exhibit *more* sexist behaviors.

THE "THERE IS NO SEXISM" GUY

Then there are men who don't believe sexism is even real.

These men exhibit *the most* sexist behaviors. Good times.

Bottom line: Men who can examine their internalized sexism behave in a way that is more empathetic to women's experiences. They generally act much less like sexist jerks and much more like Superman. Make sense?

This same concept can be applied to racism. The first step to understanding race better is to be OK with the fact that we're all a little racist. Only when we understand this can we learn to mitigate the impact of our internalized racism.

Giving Up "Woke" and Embracing "Woking"

Once you give in to the fact that you carry internalized racism and can never fully be "enlightened," the next step is learning to think of race as an ongoing journey of learning and growing. In the words of Dr. Nunn, "Developing racial consciousness and doing antiracist work requires a commitment to authentic daily reflections and awakenings. You're never done, but the journey is transformative."

This brings me to why I wrote this chapter: I think the word "woke," when used by a White person, actually perpetuates racism because it implies that our work on race is done. When we haven't lived someone's life, our journey to understand their experience will never end, and it shouldn't. That's why, if you must use a term to describe your commitment to antiracist work, I prefer the term "woking."

A brilliant way to understand why woke is a harmful term was given to me by my dear friend Ria Burns-Wilder, a rock singer and writer who makes a living in NYC as a street artist.[3]

After reading a draft of this book, Ria said this:

> As a Latinx woman, I can only say THIS IS SO TRUE! My friend Brian Patrick Burke, a White cis male and phenomenal guitarist and fiddler who many would consider a master, says that in his opinion, "everyone has to recognize their own racism. It's like music, you can't learn anything once you've decided you've mastered the instrument." If you think that you are not racist, you stop letting yourself see your more ugly inner-thoughts. If you can't admit the ugliness, you can't learn from it and you definitely can't correct it.

This is an absolutely perfect analogy. As with any skill, there can never be an "I'm done" mentality when it comes to race. We all have ugly thoughts. If we accept them, we can control them better and we can continue to learn.

In summary: White people, let's not declare ourselves woke. We are not. There is no need to prove how enlightened we are to anyone. Instead, let's model being open about learning and growing on issues of race. We really don't need more foke people. We need more woking people, lifelong students of the messy but beautiful human condition. They eat a lot of humble pie every day and are always growing, learning, and changing. By extension, they help the world grow, learn, and change. And that's really the most "woke" thing you can do.

CREATING SAFE
SPACES FOR ALL

I said in part 2 you can't claim space with a one-woman army. You also can't fight a war to claim space when a huge chunk of your soldiers are held down by bigotry and injustice.

So, how can we create a space that is welcoming for all? A space where we can raise each other up?

White people created institutional racism, we perpetuate it, and we benefit from it. Did we consciously intend to do this? Are we roaming the world with calculated malice trying to hurt others? Most of us are not. Yet our intent does not matter. The blame for racism lies firmly at the feet of White folks. Therefore, if our goal is unity among all women, White women must put in the work to dismantle White supremacy.

One way White women perpetuate racism is by inadvertently creating and maintaining unsafe spaces for our BIPOC sisters. We need to change this.

To be clear, I'm not talking about taking over movements run by BIPOCs. Far from it. When it comes to movements like Black Lives Matter, our job is to stand in support but let our sisters run those spaces. Far too often White folks have a tendency to take over when we really should step back.

I'm talking about helping our sisters of color claim space when, for whatever reason, they are not able to do so. We can't claim space when some of us do not feel safe in the spaces we inhabit.

But how do we create spaces that are truly welcoming for all to claim?

Kenneth Jones and Tema Okun do an excellent job of outlining how to create such a space in *Dismantling Racism: A Workbook for Social Change Groups*.[1] I have used their brilliant research to highlight five ways to create spaces that are welcoming and safe for all to claim.

1. **Slow it down.** Americans tend to like fast and furious, particularly in the workplace. When things are going quickly, it's very hard to work on issues of dismantling White supremacy. This is a complex and difficult issue that takes careful and measured time and attention. If you run the show in your office, try not to rush all the time. Make space for slow and thoughtful reflection.

2. **Welcome discomfort.** As explored in part 3, much of the world is centered on being nice and polite. This means not dropping big impolitic truth bombs. Unfortunately, White folks perpetuating microaggressions often are not doing so consciously. At the same time, no matter how gently delivered, any talk of race can feel like a big impolitic truth bomb to White folks. For this reason, it's important not to value politeness or protecting people's feelings over the truth. Let's put a premium on straightforward, constructive feedback, even if that feedback makes White people uncomfortable.

3. **Embrace gray.** Good and bad, black and white, right and wrong, hopefully you know why this is important from chapter 15. Understanding it's about perspective, not rightness, is critical to creating safe spaces. We need to stop thinking in extremes, otherwise known as "all or nothing" thinking, and embrace shades of gray.

4. **Cede power.** White people are traditionally in power. If it's hoarded, it will probably remain in White hands. When White people hoard power at home or in the workplace, we almost always are not creating antiracist spaces. When we declare control over a space, we are actually claiming our own space to the detriment of others. You can't hoard power if you want to rise up with others.

5. **Encourage imagination.** Again, this goes back to the idea that there is one truth. If you follow this route of thinking, usually that one "objective" truth is the truth established by the White power structure. (I'm talking "truth" in history, in the news, in our stories.) Remember, if we live in different worlds, we are experiencing different realities. Be open to the fact that you may be in the same space but you are allowed to claim it quite differently.

White Women, We Do This for Our Sisters

Here are fifteen things White women can do to make a difference (let's be the solution and rise up together!):

1. Let go of absolutes.

2. Hire women of color.

3. Question everything.

4. Interrupt microaggressions.

5. Listen to women of color.

6. Donate to, and vote for, antiracist causes.

7. Believe women of color.

8. Champion people of all genders doing antiracist work.

9. Know when to shut up and when to speak up.

10. Promote antiracist workplace policies and legislation.

11. Acknowledge, accept, and work on your internalized racism.

12. Hear feedback without defensiveness.

13. Keep a sense of humor and an open heart.

14. Attend antiracist protests that center BIPOC voices and are driven by leaders of color, such as those organized by Black Lives Matter.

15. Know that antiracist work is a marathon of persistence, not just a sprint of occasional outrage.

Claiming Space by Ceding Space

I thought a lot about how to close the final section of the final chapter of this book. What could I say? The last section . . . I wanted it to do so many things!

I wanted to share with you, dear reader . . .

* the beauty of mentorship;

* the magic that happens when we create spaces for all to speak safely;

* the empowerment we experience when our sisters feel truly heard, seen, and believed;

* the importance of claiming space together as women;

* the trust you will build if you examine your own Whiteness;

* the importance, and the possibility, of what can happen when White women really commit to doing antiracist work.

Then I realized, "Wow. That's really White of me." I wanted to do all of those things, as I am a White woman. And yet, I missed the most important thing! Somehow I forgot that when we claim space together, we all rise higher.

I am a Cook House Fellow at Cornell University. This gives me the opportunity to mentor brilliant young people at Cornell. One of my favorite experiences with being a fellow is inviting young

women to my house to sit around my kitchen counter and just ...
talk. I *think* I've taught them a few things. I *know* they've taught
me more. In our last meeting, they formed a new text thread titled
"Convos In The Kitchen." We have stayed in touch, much to my
delight. I have watched as they soared, despite carrying so many
bricks in their backpacks.

I texted them with the intention of getting some quotes and
integrating their young, knowledgeable Brown and Black voices
into this chapter. Their texted responses were so powerful that, as
usual, they reminded me of something that lies at the heart of this
chapter. That something was this: Brown and Black voices must
not amplify my voice when talking about issues of race. Their
voices must be centralized, and not through my filter. They must
claim space with their ideas and their voices.

I checked in with Dr. Nunn and told her that I had proposed to
the young women that I simply reprint their texts and give their
authentic, unedited voices the last word. Was this a good idea?
Dr. Nunn's answer was this:

> You have to have the voices of young Black and Brown
> women. You couldn't do the chapter without them.
> Their voices must be listened to and heard. Black
> feminist scholars like Monique Morris, Bettina Love,
> Ruth Brown, Brittney Cooper and Kimberlé Williams
> Crenshaw have centered and highlighted the voices
> of Black girls for years. Most spaces belong to White
> people. You need to make this their space.

So with that, I give you the words of four brilliant young
women; their advice to you and their bios are unedited by
me. Listen to what they have to say. Believe them. Insist every
woman be empowered to claim space equally and without apology. Commit to helping our sisters claim space. If we do, our
individual power and our unshakable unity will transform the
world.

CHANDLER PALMER

"What I wish a white woman would remember is that her whiteness can overpower her identity of being a woman, and for that, it makes her more powerful compared to a black woman. Acknowledge your whiteness, and embrace it, then use it to bring women up, regardless of race and gender, BESIDE you. Not behind you."

Chandler Palmer is a graduate of honors at Cornell University confidently working in the medical field. She is on the journey to medical school to represent not only in the obstetrics/gynecology and psychiatry fields but more black women in these specialties. Her goal is to bring education to her people so the stigma of avoidance between mental health and physical health, due to the history of the medical field's forms of systemic racism, can be fought against properly.

REBECCA JOSEPH

"Allies scream inclusion all the time, but they don't know how to properly address the discussion. To be an ally, White women must remember that they have a privilege to be seen for who they are instead of what they are perceived to be. I also wish that White women would remember there is great privilege in being a White woman. White women are protected because they are both White and women. They are not asked nearly as much to choose in between their race and gender. However, it is never okay for Black women to stand with BOTH their race and their gender. In fact, Black women are persecuted because of their duality and live in a world that sees us only in singularity."

Rebecca Joseph is currently a first-year law student at Brooklyn Law School. She is a Cornell University class of 2019 graduate. At Cornell, Rebecca majored in American Studies and Africana Studies while minoring in Law & Society, History, as well as Minority, Indigenous, and Third World Studies. Once she finishes law school, she intends to become an entertainment law attorney. One of her many goals is to highlight and assist in bringing diversity to the legal field as a Black woman.

GENESIS A. HEREBIA

"Stop apologizing. I am not here to grant you forgiveness. Own your whiteness and make space for other voices. Support women of color through action and not just cheap talk."

Genesis A. Herebia is a first-generation Latina pursing a master of science in social work at the Steve Hicks School of Social Work at The University of Texas at Austin. She is interested in social justice, mental health, and the well-being of the Latinx community and other marginalized populations. Genesis is currently working as a graduate research assistant on developing an Understanding Homelessness course for healthcare professionals.

EUNICE LALANNE

"Just LISTEN. One way to screw it up is to say 'I understand' or 'I've experienced something similar.' NOPE. As an ally, listen to our experiences, support the right causes, and like Chandler said, acknowledge that White women benefit from privileges that women of color don't.

"Make space for other voices!!"

Eunice LaLanne is currently a health policy analyst in Washington DC and is now transitioning to a career in voice acting. The things most important to her are her faith, her family, and treating every single person with respect and equity. Oh, and she loves to laugh!

CONCLUSION
Conversations in the Sunlight

Another world is not only possible; she is on her way. On a quiet day, I can hear her breathing.

—ARUNDHATI ROY

I went to my thirtieth high school reunion with one of my best friends, Sonia Smith. Sonia looks like she has everything together. And she does . . . now. But she went through a great deal when we were younger. Through quiet conversations and solitary introspection, Sonia somehow rose above the trials life had thrown at her. Today she is a judge, and a good one. She is also an exceptional human being.

After our reunion we went back to my house and sat in my kitchen. Sonia looked at me pensively. "Pam's doing really well," she said.

"I know," I said. "She seems to be really killing it!"

"Yeah," she said softly, "I'm really happy about that."

I looked at Sonia. We've known each other since seventh grade. I was at her son's birth. I bought my house from her parents over twenty years ago. Sonia was sitting in my kitchen now, but it used to be her kitchen. I know this woman, and I can tell, always, when my brainy, introverted friend has more to say. And I know better than to ask. I sipped my water.

After a while Sonia looked at me in that kind, empathetic, thoughtful way that hasn't changed since the day I met her.

"We were at this slumber party once," she said. "I think we were seniors. Someone asked if anyone in our group wasn't a virgin." Sonia looked down at her glass. "Then Sara looked at Pam and said, 'Pam! You aren't!' I still remember the look on Pam's face. After a really awful, painful silence, she said, 'That doesn't count. I didn't want to do that.'"

We sat quietly for a while. "I'm just really glad she's doing well," Sonia said again. "Really glad."

Until recently, women kept these stories to themselves—if we talked about them, it was in hushed tones in private spaces. Then in 2017, famous actresses accused media mogul Harvey Weinstein of sexual misconduct. Soon after, actress Alyssa Milano tweeted the hashtag #MeToo, and a powerful movement was born. (Brilliant activist, and sexual abuse survivor, Tarana Burke actually coined the phrase Me Too in 2006. It's critical to note that Burke, a Black woman, is often not credited as the mother of Me Too.) With #MeToo, a movement was born that lifted some of the shame off of sexual harassment and assault. Women took these conversations out of the darkness. It was transformative. So many of us looked around, no longer ashamed, and said, "Me too!" and our sisters stood beside us in solidarity, each individual story creating an unstoppable army of support.

"Never again," we said with steely determination. Together, we would make the world do things differently. And we did. #MeToo was a bloodless revolution. It wasn't fought with guns, but with stories, stories born from pain, pouring out of our hearts with the fury of a dam breaking. The battle isn't over, but things have changed radically, and they have changed forever. Our collective voices, courage, and demand for change have made it so.

This book was originally inspired by the ad hoc talks I had with women in hushed tones in the safety of the bathroom after my talks. We would chat about their professional lives at first, but it always became so much more. When we finally left the bathroom, I would *know* these women—and I would invariably hear this refrain, "It really sucks that we have to have these conversations in the bathroom."

The bathroom is one of the safest spaces for most women. I say "most" because as I noted at the beginning of this book, our trans sisters often are not welcome there. That special space must be for them what it is for so many women: a refuge. And it is such a special space. Think about it. If you were walking down the street and saw a woman crying quietly to herself, would you stop and ask her what was wrong? Probably not. If you saw that same woman in the bathroom, you can bet you would ask, and you can bet a really raw, honest conversation would ensue. We cry in the bathroom, we confide in each other in the bathroom, we gripe about unfairness in the bathroom, we express our buried anger in the bathroom. The bathroom is the one space we fear no judgment from men. It is where we speak our truth.

And this is a problem. This is why things are changing at a snail's pace. This is why, as fierce as she is, I still fear for my daughter.

Darkness perpetuates shame and fear. It isolates, silences, and makes us small. Living in a world where half of the population fears speaking their truth unless they are huddled together, talking quietly, out of earshot of the other half of the population, isn't just problematic. It's damaging. It's not just damaging for women. It's damaging for everyone.

When we speak in whispers, when we mute our stories out of fear or sometimes deny our more painful realities altogether, we allow others to frame the narrative of our lives. I wrote this book to empower women so they could wield the most powerful arsenal we have: our truth. If we are to be kind, brave, just, visible, and united, we must tell our stories. Our stories define our history, frame our present, and pave the way for our future. If we can shape women's narratives, our truth can change the world.

Let's take our conversations out of the darkness of the bathroom.

Let's use our voices to speak truth to power, shine light on our experiences, and demand change.

We are not alone. We have important stories to tell. Let's tell them.

These conversations will be scary at first, but think of #MeToo. The more we stand firm in our power and speak without apology, the more women will follow. More importantly, we don't need to be unafraid to have those conversations and make those demands. We just need to be brave. Bravery—despite the line we have been fed since the time we were little, since we read stories about fairy tales with princes and princesses—is not the lack of fear. It is action in the face of fear. There is nothing brave about acting without fear. You're either reckless or your action doesn't warrant the grand title of bravery. I said it in my TEDx, and I'll say it again. *Bravery is not a lack of fear. Bravery is being terrified and doing what you need to do anyway.*

WOMEN HAVE ALWAYS HAD TO BE BRAVE.

We wake up in the morning when we're tired, but get our kids to school and go to work.

We lead Fortune 500 companies, companies that were once exclusively run by men.

We live in rural and urban poverty and never went to college, yet we sacrifice for years to make sure our children can go.

We lead movements when our children are murdered by police.

We help Americans fly into space.

We help our best friends fly when they're down.

We get up after being assaulted.

We stand up for other women.

We stand up for ourselves, leaving abusive relationships.

We love who we want to love.

We tell our daughters they can be whoever they want to be.

We tell ourselves the same.

Women are the face of bravery.

Fear tells us that something is worth doing, that there are stakes worth fighting for. Listen to your fear, but don't let it stop you from claiming space.

I have been afraid every single last time I've done something I've been proud of. Leaving law school? Scary. Anticipating child-birth? Fear beyond words. Starting my acting studio? Terrifying. Getting a divorce? Bone chilling. Giving my first talk? Panic inducing. Writing this book? Yep. But what I have learned about myself is that despite the fact that I scare easily, I don't quit easily. My fear does not rule me. My grit does, and so does my belief that even if I fall down, I can and will get back up again. And in those moments when my resolve falters, when fear almost wins, I have an army of exceptional women in my life who remind me in no uncertain terms that I have to push through, despite my fear. They remind me that I am brave.

Let's have brave conversations in the sunlight.

Be afraid. Be terrified. Let our voices shake. But never, never let fear silence us, never apologize for being the rule-breaking, rule-making badass/superhero/boss ladies that we are. Not once. Not ever. We bow to no one. We make ourselves small for no one.

And now, Wonder Woman, grab your space-claiming cape and go save your own life.

Turn around, reach out your hand, and lift up your sisters.

We are brave. We got this.

NOTES

Chapter 1

1 "3 Surprising Risks of Poor Posture," Harvard Health Publishing, September 2018, *https://www.health.harvard.edu/staying-healthy/3-surprising-risks-of-poor-posture*.

Chapter 2

1 Leo Taylor, telephone interview by the author, June 8, 2020.

Chapter 3

1 "Deborah Gruenfeld: Power & Influence," Stanford Graduate School of Business, March 13, 2013, YouTube video, 20:50, *https://www.youtube.com/watch?v=KdQHAeAnHmw*.

2 Simone Kühn et al., "Why Do I Like You When You Behave like Me? Neural Mechanisms Mediating Positive Consequences of Observing Someone Being Imitated," *Social Neuroscience* 5, no. 4 (2010): 384–92, *https://doi.org/10.1080/17470911003633750*.

3 Vanessa Van Edwards, "Mirroring Body Language: 4 Steps to Successfully Mirror Others," Science of People, April 20, 2020, *https://www.scienceofpeople.com/mirroring/*.

Part 2 Introduction

1 Ilene H. Lang and Reggie Van Lee, "Institutional Investors Must Help Close the Race and Gender Gaps in Venture Capital," *Harvard Business Review*, August 27, 2020, *https://hbr.org/2020/08/institutional-investors-must-help-close-the-race-and-gender-gaps-in-venture-capital*.

Chapter 4

1   Victor Lipman, "Study: Narcissists Do Best in Job Interviews," *Psychology Today*, July 15, 2014, *https://www.psychologytoday.com/us/blog/mind -the-manager/201407/study-narcissists-do-best-in-job-interviews*.

2   C. G. Jung, *Memories, Dreams, Reflections* (New York: HarperCollins, 1995); John Bradshaw, *Homecoming: Reclaiming and Championing Your Inner Child* (New York: Bantam Books, 1990).

Chapter 5

1   "Domestic Violence Statistics," National Domestic Abuse Hotline, *https://www.thehotline.org/resources/statistics/*.

Chapter 6

1   Kira Sholeen Wagner, telephone discussion with author, June 19, 2020.

Part 3 Introduction

1   Lexico.com, s.v. "nice," accessed April 2020, *https://www.lexico.com/en /definition/nice*.

2   *American Heritage Dictionary*, s.v. "kind," accessed April 2020, *https:// ahdictionary.com/word/search.html?q=kind*.

Chapter 8

1   Lexico.com, s.v. "feminism," accessed April 2020, *https://www.lexico .com/en/definition/feminism.*

2   "Legal Case: Elizabeth Johnson, Massachusetts Bay, December 5, 1642," Colonial America: The Age of Sodomitical Sin, OutHistory, accessed May 2020, *http://outhistory.org/exhibits/show/the-age-of -sodomitical-sin/1640s/legal-case-elizabeth-johnson-m*.

3   "History of Sodomy Laws and the Strategy That Led Up to Today's Decision," ACLU, accessed 2020, *https://www.aclu.org/other/history -sodomy-laws-and-strategy-led-todays-decision*.

4   "2018 Hate Crime Statistics: Table 1 Incidents, Offenses, Victims, and Known Offenders by Bias Motivation, 2018," Criminal Justice Information Services Division, FBI, 2019, *https://ucr.fbi.gov/hate-crime/2018 /tables/table-1.xls*.

5   Susan Miller, "'Shocking' Numbers: Half of LGBTQ Adults Live in
    States Where No Laws Ban Job Discrimination," *USA Today*, October
    8, 2019, *https://www.usatoday.com/story/news/nation/2019/10/08/lgbt
    -employment-discrimination-half-of-states-offer-no-protections/
    3837244002/*.

6   Nicole Pasulka, "The 'Criminal' Black Lesbian: Where Does This Dam-
    aging Stereotype Come From?," *Code Switch*, March 17, 2016, *https://
    www.npr.org/sections/codeswitch/2016/03/17/456541972/the-criminal
    -black-lesbian-where-does-this-damaging-stereotype-come-from*.

7   Mary E. Asmus, Tieneke Ritmeester, and Ellen L. Pence, "Prosecuting
    Domestic Abuse Cases in Duluth: Developing Effective Prosecution
    Strategies from Understanding the Dynamics of Abusive Relation-
    ships," *Hamline Law Review* 15, no. 1 (1991): 115–166.

8   Caroline Heldman, Meredith Conroy, and Alissa Ackerman, *Sex and
    Gender in the 2016 Presidential Election* (Santa Barbara, CA: Praeger,
    2018), 261.

9   "WATCH: Verbal Assault against Women 'Not New. And That Is the
    Problem,' Rep. Ocasio-Cortez Says," *PBS NewsHour*, YouTube video,
    10:11, July, 23 2020, *https://www.youtube.com/watch?v=kjEhiyvljxU*.

Part 4 Introduction

1   Dr. Nia Nunn, telephone interview by author, June 2020.

Chapter 10

1   Robin Bleiweis, "Quick Facts about the Gender Wage Gap," Center for
    American Progress, March 24, 2020, *https://www.americanprogress.org
    /issues/women/reports/2020/03/24/182141/quick-facts-gender-wage-gap/*.

2   Olga Khazan, "Nearly Half of All Murdered Women Are Killed by
    Romantic Partners," July 24, 2017, *https://www.theatlantic.com/health
    /archive/2017/07/homicides-women/534306/*.

3   Suzanne C. Swan, "More Than a Myth: Drink Spiking Happens,"
    American Psychological Association, May 24, 2016. *https://www.apa
    .org/news/press/releases/2016/05/drink-spiking*.

Chapter 11

1   Dr. Kiranjit Bali, Zoom interview by author, June 23, 2020.

2 "Facts About Sexual Harassment," U.S. Equal Employment Opportunity Commission, 2020, *https://www.eeoc.gov/fact-sheet/facts-about-sexual-harassment*.

3 W. Timothy Coombs and Sherry J. Holladay, "Understanding the Aggressive Workplace: Development of the Workplace Aggression Tolerance Questionnaire," *Communication Studies* 55, no. 3 (May 2009), *https://doi.org/10.1080/10510970409388633*.

4 S. Einarsen, ed., et al., *Bullying and Harassment in the Workplace. Theory, Research and Practice* (Boca Raton, FL: CRC press, 2000).

5 S. Einarsen, H. Hoel, and G. Notelaers, "Measuring Exposure to Bullying in the Workplace: Development and Validity for the Revised Negative Acts Questionnaire," *Work and Stress* 23 (2009): 24–44.

6 Fons Naus, Ad van Iterson, and Robert Roe, "Organizational Cynicism: Extending the Exit, Voice, Loyalty, and Neglect Model of Employees' Responses to Adverse Conditions in the Workplace," *Human Relations* 60, no. 5 (2007): 683–718, *https://doi.org/10.1177/0018726707079198*.

Chapter 12

1 "Cultural Considerations: What Are Microaggressions?" Inside CASA, Texas CASA, February 19, 2019, *https://texascasa.org/cultural-considerations-what-are-microaggressions/*.

2 D. W. Sue, et al., "Racial Microaggressions in Everyday Life: Implications for Clinical Practice," *The American Psychologist* 62, no. 4 (2007): 271–86, *https://doi.org/10.1037/0003-066X.62.4.271*.

Chapter 13

1 Kieran Snyder, "Boys Learn to Interrupt. Girls Learn to Shut Up.," *Slate*, August 14, 2014, *https://slate.com/human-interest/2014/08/child-interruption-study-boys-learn-to-interrupt-girls-as-young-as-4-years-old.html*.

Chapter 16

1 "Perpetrators of Sexual Violence: Statistics," RAINN, accessed October 28, 2020, *https://www.rainn.org/statistics/perpetrators-sexual-violence*.

2 Jennifer L. Berdahl and Celia Moore, "Workplace Harassment: Double Jeopardy for Minority Women," *Journal of Applied Psychology* 91, no. 2 (2006): 426–436, *https://doi.org/10.1037/0021-9010.91.2.426*.

3   Ian Thomsen, "The Research Is Clear: White People Are Not More Likely than Black People to Be Killed by Police," News@Northeastern, July 16, 2020, *https://news.northeastern.edu/2020/07/16/the-research-is-clear -white-people-are-not-more-likely-than-black-people-to-be-killed-by-police/*.

4   Judith Warner, Nora Ellmann, and Diana Boesch, "The Women's Leadership Gap," Center for American Progress, November 20, 2018, *https:// www.americanprogress.org/issues/women/reports/2018/11/20/461273 /womens-leadership-gap-2/*.

5   Courtney Connley, "New Census Data Reveals No Progress Has Been Made on Closing the Overall Gender Pay Gap," CNBC Make It, September 18, 2020, *https://www.cnbc.com/2020/09/18/new-census-data -reveals-no-progress-has-been-made-closing-the-gender-pay-gap.html*.

6   Emily Badger et al., "Extensive Data Shows Punishing Reach of Racism for Black Boys," *New York Times*, March 19, 2018, *https://www.nytimes. com/interactive/2018/03/19/upshot/race-class-white-and-black-men.html*.

Chapter 17

1   Nicola Kirkpatrick, "The Good, the Bad, the Ugly: Why Attractive People Are Successful," Betterhelp, April 13, 2018, *https://www .betterhelp.com/advice/general/the-good-the-bad-the ugly-why-attractive -people-are-successful/*.

Chapter 18

1   Juana Summers, "Obama Says Democrats Don't Always Need to Be 'Politically Woke,'" NPR, October 31, 2019, *https://www.npr.org/2019 /10/31/774918215/obama-says-democrats-dont-always-need-to-be -politically-woke*.

2   *Merriam-Webster*, s.v. "woke," accessed June 17, 2020, *https://www .merriam-webster.com/dictionary/woke*.

3   Ria Burnes Wilder, telephone and text interview by author, August 18, 2020.

Chapter 19

1   Kenneth Jones and Tema Okun, *Dismantling Racism: A Workbook for Social Change Groups*, ChangeWork, 2001, *https://www .dismantlingracism.org/*.

ACKNOWLEDGMENTS

You Can't Claim Space with a One-Woman Army

So many women bravely shared their questions, truths, and hearts with me in homes, classrooms, and audiences throughout the world. (And bathrooms!)

Your journey was my classroom.

***

This book was a collaborative effort born from an army of fierce, loving, collaborative, independent, creative, pragmatic, disruptive, disciplined, knowledgeable, talented, and supportive space claimers.

With deepest gratitude, I thank you.

You each made a difference.

Family Fabulousness

My parents—Thys VanCort and Beth Prentice, your generous, thoughtful, and loving support made this possible.

My kids—my daughter and sons, Ella, Jonah, and Lucian Mead-VanCort, and my nephew Eric Cuadrado. I love you beyond words. This is for you, extraordinary ones, and for your engaged friends I so admire. Your generation is already changing the world.

Editorial Enchantress

Anna Leinberger—wise, patient, edifying, fierce editor! You saw the potential, then used your magical, transformative powers! This is *our* book. Thank you, rock star, space-claiming soul sister!

Purposeful Publishers

Berrett-Koehler—I am beyond grateful. Thanks for taking a chance on me.

Adroit Artists

Lynn Buckley—your cover design/illustrations are game changing. Your collaborative artistry and friendship are gifts.

Barbara Ann Jordan—she shot the cover photo—badassery!

My talented seventeen-year-old son took my bio picture. Lucian, you make me proud.

Edward Wade—My incredibly talented design and production guru, with the patience of Job!

Foreword Ferociousness

Alma Derricks—honored to know you, my sister. Thanks for brilliantly claiming space with me like a damn boss.

Magnificent Manifesters

These folks amplify voices with conviction, integrity, caring, and class.

Mark Fortier, Jessica Pellien, Mariah Dwyer (Fortier), and Ken Sterling (Big Speak), thank you.

Amanda Colbert, Ashley Dos Santos, and Chris Zilles (social media/communication media gurus!)

Dangerous (Book) Doulas—The CFB Sisters

This ferocious CFB Sisterhood shared wonderful editorial feedback.

Prof. Sarah Jefferis (original CFB editor!)

Maureen Forys (creative designer) and Susan Berge (collaborative/ brilliant copy editor!)

Kiana Chow (footnote madness!)

Marissa Accordino, Liz Bassano, Kate Buckley, Ria Burns-Wilder, Tracy Habecker, Judge Maura Kennedy-Smith, Melissa Levy, Prof. Cynthia Henderson, Rachel Hocket, Misty Monroe, Kieren Munson-Burke, Melissa Sawyer, Suzan Senovich, Katie Spallone, Leah Summers, Jamie Swinnerton, Dr. Saskya Van Nouhuys, and Kira Sholeen Wagner (coined "book doula")

Cartooned Collaborators

You fun, artistic, fearless humans, let's keep creating together.

Sister/partner Katie Spallone, nieces Kieren and Mirana Munson-Burke, superheroes Mike Donato and Paige Anderson, collaborators Alek Osinski, Steve Olenski, Lynn Buckley, Tyree Cobbins, Darryle Johnson, and David Kossack, earth shakers/ change makers Rep. Leslyn Mc Bean-Clairborne, Prachi Ruina, and my inspiring daughter, Annabella Mead-VanCort

Disruptive Didacts

You help all genders intersectionally claim space. Thank you for lending your knowledge and wisdom to the book.

Dr. Kiranjit Bali, Dr. Dolly Chugh, Dr. Nia Nunn, Dr. Leo Taylor, and Kim Munson-Burke, MSW

Early Enthusiasts

My first guides, connectors, and advocates. Forever thankful.

Allison McLean, Megan Ahern, and Will Weisser

Kitchen Convo Courageousness

When you mentor, the benefits are endless. These women are my teachers.

Rebecca Joseph, Genesis A. Herebia, Eunice LaLanne, Chandler Palmer, Jodi Robertson, and Jeannie Yamazaki (Dean Shorna Allred, thanks for the Cook House Fellowship and Emeka Ojukwu . . . our group!)

Amplifying Advocates

Accomplished space-claiming endorsers:

Octavia Abell, Prof. Andrew Chignell, Dr. Dolly Chugh, Assoc. Dean Dionetta Jones Crayton, Joe Desena, Prof. Christine Guest, Assoc. Dean Sara Xayarath Hernández, Misty Monroe, Kyleigh Russ, Suzan Senovich

Righteous Revolutionaries

When I want to quit, I look to them for inspirational guidance. Then, I dust myself off and claim space. Thank you, teachers.

Dr. Maya Angelou, Supreme Court justices Ruth Bader Ginsburg and Sonia Sotomayor, Oprah Winfrey, VP Kamala Harris, Rep. Alexandria Ocasio-Cortez, Gloria Steinem, Eartha Kitt, Emma Watson, Prof. bell hooks, Sec. Hillary Rodham Clinton, Duchess Meghan Markle, Dr. Anita Hill, Audre Lorde, Dr. Angela Davis, Madeleine L'Engle, Geena Davis, Angelina Jolie, Lizzo, Bonnie Raitt, Whoopi Goldberg, Prof. Kimberlé Williams Crenshaw, Dr. Robin DiAngelo, Rep. Barbara Jordan, Sen. Elizabeth Warren, Stevie Wonder, and . . . Wonder Woman!

Valorous Villagers

It takes a village, and the world needs more inspiring CFB villages like this one. Thank you.

Nancy Beck and family, Arthur Bicknell, Mike Buchanan, Liz Cohen, Sam Cohen, Jennifer Stage Christenson, Dr. Norma Cooney, Prof. Cathy Lee Crane, Jesse Crawford, William Cunningham, Jamie Donnelly, Clayton Duban, Sarah Evanega, Ben Furnace, Mike and Emma Ellis, Ross Haarstad, Jason, Chris and Hayden, Mona Gracen, Alice Green, Phil Gushee, Prof. Christine Guest, Raquel Gonzalez, Max Della Pia, Rep. Anna Kelles, David Kossack, Jessica Hanna, Polly Holmberg, Darryle Johnson, Dr. Jeff Lewis, Julie MacMillin, Ellen McCollister, Josh Mack, Dr. John-Paul Mead (friend/father to my kids!), Josh Neuman, Professors Robert & Anne Marie Pois, Dr. Chandra Muller, George Sapio, Amanda Setton, Dep. Provost John Siliciano, Frank Storace, Maura Stephens, Steve Messa, Daniel Masciari (forever collaborator), Okoro Munn, Dr. James Smith, Mayor Svante Myrick, Amy Kay Raymond, Dr. Anne Sisson Runyan, Christopher Teitelbaum, Jeremy Webb, Roberta Wallitt, Dean Warnick, Jeff Williams, Peter Wolfram, Chris Zilles, the Munson-Burkes, VanCorts, Prentices, extended DeMao family, "The Gang," Alliance for Science Fellows (changing the world!), '89, and my supportive FB, arts, Ithaca and Cornell University communities

Fearsome Finishers

Steve—you have such a big, mighty, and beautiful heart. Oh, how it touched mine. Thank you for . . . all of it.

Alek Osinski—my brother, your support, belief in me, and editing genius prove that every gender can be a badass intersectional CFB. You wear it well.

Mary Louise Marini VanCort—Mom, you told me I could do anything. You told me to "be great" every time we said goodbye. You might as well have been saying, "Go claim some space, my daughter. I know you can." You may still be missing, but you live in my heart. Wherever you are, know that I listened. I hope you're proud of me.

INDEX

ABOUT THE AUTHOR

PHOTO BY LUCIAN MEAD-VANCORT

Eliza VanCort is an in-demand speaker and writer on communications, career and workplace issues, and women's empowerment. The founder of The Actor's Workshop of Ithaca, she is also a Cook House Fellow at Cornell University, an advisory board member of the Performing Arts for Social Change, a Diversity Crew partner, and a member of Govern for America's League of Innovators.

Eliza has given acclaimed talks to diverse groups like Microsoft, Cornell, MIT, The World Artists United Music Conference, TEDx, and Girl Up. She is a parent of four kids and loves cycling and conversations in her kitchen. She will never turn down quality chocolate.

A Woman's Guide to Claiming Space

Stand Tall. Raise Your Voice. Be Heard.

If you don't claim space for yourself, you will NEVER be able to lift up another human. And if we claim space for ourselves but also for each other, we will build a better world for all of us.

That is the critical message I hope you take away from this book. We are all sisters. We MUST raise each other up, because when we rise together, we rise higher. I've included this discussion with that goal, to facilitate learning, either on your own, or with your sisters.

One of the most powerful ways to create change is to stand in our truths, speak our minds, and hear the stories of our sisters. Coming out of the shadows and sharing our ideas and experiences remains one of the most powerful ways women can create change. An act of bravery, it frees us to own our power, and in turn claims more space collectively in our rapidly changing world. So go grab your sisters, turn on the kettle or crack open a bottle of wine, and start the conversation! The time to claim space is now.

Warmly,
Eliza

Questions for Discussion

1. Claiming Space. This is an idea that will mean something different to every woman, evoking in each person a unique perspective. To some it comes naturally, and to others can seem like an inaccessible superpower. What's your definition of claiming space?

2. In the book, I tell stories from my childhood. Formative early experiences convinced me that claiming space was an unsafe thing to do. What messages do you remember learning as a child about ceding or claiming space? Did you relate to any of mine? Did you receive a different set of messages?

3. Claiming space is not just about physicality and voice. There are five dimensions of claiming space: Claiming Physical Space, Claiming Space Collaboratively, Refusal to Cede Space, Claiming Safety in Any Space, and

Claiming Space in Unity. How did you feel about these five dimensions? Which areas do you already feel confident in? Which dimensions do you feel you learned the most about and want to work on?

4.   If claiming space were easy, everyone would do it, and no one would need this book! Many narratives tell women "If only you negotiated more, the wage gap would disappear" or "Women don't get promoted because you don't ask," but we know that's a pretty simplistic perspective. Many women hesitate to claim space because when we've tried, we've faced consequences. Have you attempted to claim space for yourself (in any of the five dimensions!) and experienced backlash? How did you deal with it? What has been the collective impact of those moments on your life and subsequent choices?

Dimension 1: Claim Physical Space

5.   Do a self-assessment: How do you move through space? How do you hold your body? Where do you tend to look? When you enter a room, where do you gravitate to?

6.   A book club is a fantastic opportunity to try some of the physicality and voice exercises:
   a. Try video recording each other (or yourself, if you are flying solo) giving a short talk, or even just reading a poem out loud.
   Then, as a group, do the posture correcting exercises from pages 21–27.
   Afterward, video each other / yourself again with the same text, intentionally employing the posture corrections. See the difference!

   b. Do something similar with voice: record each other reading the same text several different times, changing the locations of the lifts and the drops. How does this change the impact of your words?

   c. Try the group exercise on page 53 to practice playing high and low behaviors. Discuss when in your lives it would be appropriate to make use of these tactics.

Dimension 2: Claim Space Collaboratively

7.   Did you relate to the discussion of anti-mentors? Are you now able to see anti-mentors in your life? How do they make you feel small? What steps can you take to redefine your boundaries and neutralize their negative impact?

8. Within your group, or within a set timeframe if you are reading this solo, come up with three ways that you can support each other's personal or professional goals. Make an actionable plan and follow through!

Dimension 3: Never Cede Your Space

9. Poll the room: Who has been called Crazy, Feminist, Bitch, or all three? What do these words mean to you? What is your relationship to them? Do they make you feel even smaller? Or do they make you feel powerful and determined? How will you react to name calling now that you have read the book?

10. What sorts of scenarios put pressure on you to make yourself small, to cede your space to the priorities or values of others? Why do you think you react in this way to these situations?

11. The world often punishes women for having and enforcing our boundaries. Share scenarios in which you have attempted to enforce a boundary that was not respected. What can you do to protect this boundary in the future? How can you make, enforce, and push back on people who resist your boundaries?

Dimension 4: Claim Safety in Any Space

12. It's time for "Claim Safety Bingo!" In your group, take a few moments to brainstorm examples from your life when you have experienced space-thievery: anger, bullying, sexual harassment, microaggressions, mansplaining, interruptions. Listen to those in the group who want to share their stories. Think about the experiences similar to your own. How can you use what you've learned in the book to show up for each other?

13. If you can meet several times to discuss the book, try out some of the tools and tactics between meetings. For example, try combatting interruptions one week and microaggressions the next. You might even agree on a specific one or two to try out as a group. Then regroup later to compare notes on how your experiments played out. What happened? How did people react? What did you learn?

Dimension 5: Claim Space in Unity

14. Let's talk chapter 15: The Need to Be Right Will Cause You to Do Wrong. First take a deep breath, and spend a few moments considering

any apprehension you feel about making mistakes. Why are you afraid to be wrong? What are some of the consequences? How can "Feel, Think, Act" help you to challenge this damaging habit?

15. As a group, play the invisible backpack game: First review chapter 17: Understand What You Were Given. What's in your backpack? Where was your starting point? What is NOT in your backpack? How does it feel to see each other's bricks? How can we climb together more fairly?

16. Take the "Are You Foke?" quiz in chapter 18. Unless you are a woman of color, you are foke! (Surprise!) No, but seriously, what did this bring up for you? If you are a woman of color, what would you have added to the quiz?

17. What have you learned from part 5? Do you see the world differently now? Are there things you wished had been included that were not? If you are White, did you have a reaction to not being centralized?

18. What uplifted you most in the book? How are you best situated to claim space for yourself, and for your sisters? Develop an action plan together to claim that space, and then go do it!

Berrett–Koehler
Publishers

Berrett-Koehler is an independent publisher dedicated to an ambitious mission: *Connecting people and ideas to create a world that works for all.*

Our publications span many formats, including print, digital, audio, and video. We also offer online resources, training, and gatherings. And we will continue expanding our products and services to advance our mission.

We believe that the solutions to the world's problems will come from all of us, working at all levels: in our society, in our organizations, and in our own lives. Our publications and resources offer pathways to creating a more just, equitable, and sustainable society. They help people make their organizations more humane, democratic, diverse, and effective (and we don't think there's any contradiction there). And they guide people in creating positive change in their own lives and aligning their personal practices with their aspirations for a better world.

And we strive to practice what we preach through what we call "The BK Way." At the core of this approach is *stewardship,* a deep sense of responsibility to administer the company for the benefit of all of our stakeholder groups, including authors, customers, employees, investors, service providers, sales partners, and the communities and environment around us. Everything we do is built around stewardship and our other core values of *quality, partnership, inclusion,* and *sustainability.*

This is why Berrett-Koehler is the first book publishing company to be both a B Corporation (a rigorous certification) and a benefit corporation (a for-profit legal status), which together require us to adhere to the highest standards for corporate, social, and environmental performance. And it is why we have instituted many pioneering practices (which you can learn about at www.bkconnection.com), including the Berrett-Koehler Constitution, the Bill of Rights and Responsibilities for BK Authors, and our unique Author Days.

We are grateful to our readers, authors, and other friends who are supporting our mission. We ask you to share with us examples of how BK publications and resources are making a difference in your lives, organizations, and communities at www.bkconnection.com/impact.

Dear reader,

Thank you for picking up this book and welcome to the worldwide BK community! You're joining a special group of people who have come together to create positive change in their lives, organizations, and communities.

What's BK all about?

Our mission is to connect people and ideas to create a world that works for all.

Why? Our communities, organizations, and lives get bogged down by old paradigms of self-interest, exclusion, hierarchy, and privilege. But we believe that can change. That's why we seek the leading experts on these challenges—and share their actionable ideas with you.

A welcome gift

To help you get started, we'd like to offer you a **free copy** of one of our bestselling ebooks:

www.bkconnection.com/welcome

When you claim your **free ebook**, you'll also be subscribed to our blog.

Our freshest insights

Access the best new tools and ideas for leaders at all levels on our blog at ideas.bkconnection.com.

Sincerely,

Your friends at Berrett-Koehler

Certified

Corporation